Wychwoo(

The evolution of a wooded landscape

Wychwood

The evolution of
a wooded landscape

Beryl Schumer

Foreword by Harold Fox

THE WYCHWOOD PRESS

Published in 1999 by
The Wychwood Press, an imprint of Jon Carpenter Publishing
2, The Spendlove Centre, Charlbury, Oxfordshire OX7 3PQ
Tel/fax 01608 811969

An earlier edition of this book was published in 1984 by Leicester University Press under the title *The Evolution of Wychwood to 1400: Pioneers, Frontiers and Forests*. For the new edition, the text has been revised throughout, and illustrations and a new Chapter 6 have been added

The illustration on p37 is reproduced by permission of The British Library (BL ADD MS 6027 (1617, John Nordern The Elder and The Younger))

ISBN 1 902279 02 6

Printed in England by J. W. Arrowsmith Ltd., Bristol
Cover printed by KMS Litho, Hook Norton

Contents

Tables

Notes on usage

In this book, the word Forest is used in its legal sense, as signifying an area of land under Forest Law.

'Medieval' is used for the period from 1066 to approximately AD 1400.

'Vill' is used to denote an economic unit consisting of a settlement with its fields, meadows, pastures etc., which does not of itself form a manor or parish.

The settlements of Ascott-under-Wychwood, Milton-under-Wychwood and Shipton-under-Wychwood will, for convenience, be referred to as Ascott, Milton and Shipton. (The earliest appearance of the suffix is AD 1280, so this in fact agrees with the early medieval usage.) The vills of Minster Lovell and Stanton Harcourt will be referred to as Minster and Stanton, since in the Middle Ages the suffixes referred only to the Lovell and Harcourt manors in those vills.

See also the Glossary on pages 90-91.

Foreword

Woodland History

by Harold Fox

B ERYL SCHUMER's *Wychwood*, now republished, was originally entitled *The Evolution of Wychwood to 1400: Pioneers, Frontiers and Forests* and came out in 1984 as one of the Occasional Papers of the Department of English Local History at the University of Leicester. These papers — described in an obituary of Herbert Finberg, their founder, as his 'brilliant series' and by Maurice Beresford as the 'glory of Leicester University Press'[1] — have always been works of scholarship which break new ground and open up whole new fields for investigation. *The Evolution of Wychwood* did just that: its author was as pioneering as the peasants she describes breaking into the woodland and underwood to create new fields and farms and livelihoods. Along with several other works, written at more or less the same time, it began what was perhaps a new phase in the writing of woodland history.

Woodland history has a long pedigree. It begins with histories of the royal forests, their complex laws and the world of their officers — largely legal and administrative history as one would expect, though such works can still be a useful quarry for the social historian. The tradition goes back to the lawyer John Manwood's *Treatise and Discourse of the Lawes of the Forrest* published in 1598 and includes *The Royal Forests of England* by J. C. Cox (1905) in the Antiquary's Books series, still a useful and a handsome volume whose red and gilt spine gleams at me from the end of my library as I write this. Several individual royal forests had their own histories such as W. R. Fisher's *The Forest of Essex: its History, Laws, Administration and Ancient Customs* (1887) which is almost wholly concerned with administrative matters.

There was an interesting phase in the writing of woodland history, in the 1950s and 1960s, when emphasis seems to have been placed on woodland as a resource to be destroyed, tamed, converted into 'more profitable' use, a phase which of course pre-dates Swampy and notions of 'green' and of sustainability. The works of two other pioneers — in the fields of landscape history and of historical geography — illustrate the genre very well. The landscape historian was W. G. Hoskins, founder of Leicester's Department of English Local History, who, as is clear from the quotation on the first page of *Wychwood*, sometimes thought of woodland as a 'negative' type of land-use, something which had to be destroyed before fields, farmsteads and villages could be inserted in its place. He imagined, after the fashion of his time, that England was densely wooded at the beginning of the Anglo-Saxon period (later he changed his opinion) and therefore thought that much woodland clearance still remained to be done in the 250 years or so following the Norman Conquest. Of the beginning of that period he wrote, as only he could have done: 'From rising ground England must have seemed one great forest ... an almost unbroken sea of tree-tops with a thin blue spiral of smoke rising here and there at long intervals.' The section entitled 'The clearing of the woodland' in his very widely acclaimed *Making of the English Landscape* (1955) is therefore a lively and enthusiastic account of what he saw as a massive work of reclamation 'between the making of Domesday Book and the coming of the Black Death which put a decisive end to the first great wave of colonization'. The wildwood was at last 'tamed', a word recalling a sentiment which has a long tradition in the philosophical concept of a natural world which was brutal and uncouth, although Hoskins by no means subscribed to that wider view.[2] The historical geographer was H. L. Darby who was always fascinated in changes in land use leading to 'improvement', the draining of the fens, moorland reclamation and woodland clearance. He too wrote a piece called 'Clearing the wood' in which he seized upon the Anglo-Saxon poet's reference to the ploughman as the 'grey-haired enemy of the woodland' and, like Hoskins, stressed how much still needed to be destroyed in the centuries following the Norman Conquest.[3] Both scholars must have been much influenced by the great French historian Marc Bloch who wrote of the twelfth and thirteenth centuries as 'the age of large-scale clearances'.[4]

Beryl Schumer's *Wychwood* belongs to a new phase in the writing of woodland history, in which the emphasis is not upon destruction but on the management of woodland and on woodland society. In what is a hasty survey of the subject, and a highly subjective selection from the literature, it might seem wrong to single out names; but I shall nevertheless do so. P. A. J. Petit's *Royal Forests of Northamptonshire* (1968) was designed, as is clear from his introduction, as a rounded blend of legal and economic history along with study of 'the landscape of woodland' and 'its important influence on local social and economic life'. In 1969 Jean Birrell discussed woodlands as seed-beds for the emergence of crafts and craftsmen of a variety of kinds (for example, makers of glass, charcoal, wooden vessels and new and spare parts for agricultural tools and vehicles); this contribution is part of her long and distinguished series of papers on the social history of those woodlands which survived into the thirteenth century.[5] Two novel works, their emphases clearly signalled by their subtitles, were C. E. Hart's *Royal Forest: a History of Dean's Woods as Producers of Timber* (1966) and *The New Forest: an Ecological History* (1968), by C. R. Tubbs. A significant paper was Alan Everitt's of 1977, in which he showed that some English woodlands were once systematically used as pastures, in some cases by the flocks and herds of people living at a long distance from the resource.[6]

Woodland management is also a central theme of the compendious *Ancient Woodland* (1980) by Oliver Rackham, one of a number of botanists and ecologists who were realizing at the time that what they observed, in various types of surviving woodlands, was a product of centuries of conservation and human use. Unlike Hoskins and Darby, Rackham starts (in historic times at least) with England as, generally, a rather sparsely wooded country, with exceptions in some regions (one thinks, for example, of the great Andredsweald of Anglo-Saxon Sussex and Kent).

Readers of this Foreword may wonder how views on the extent of woodland could be so violently opposed as those of Hoskins and Darby on the one hand and Rackham on the other. The fact is that reconstructions of early woodland depend on interpretation of a large number of types of evidence — place-names, Domesday Book, palaeo-botanical evidence (in places), Anglo-Saxon charters, later documents — and the methods used in the manipulation of each do not constitute an exact science, so that statistics, if one is brave enough to use them, may be far from accurate. Each type can be used to produce a different view of the extent of woodland and the types may be juxtaposed and permutated in different ways. Rackham's concept of England as relatively lightly wooded in historic times immediately makes one ponder about many facets of early social history: about continuity of settlement between the Romano-British period and the beginnings of Anglo-Saxon England; about the formation of villages, which were once thought to have been a necessity among people who needed to bind themselves into 'ready made communities' in order to open up dense woodland.[7] It also makes one ponder about whether or not Bloch's idea of 'an age of large-scale clearances' is applicable to England; there are further implications for social history here because colonization is always said to have gone hand in hand with the development of personal freedom. Rackham's revelation led him not along these avenues but into the history of the conservation and management of the surviving woods. His grand theme is that relative scarcity of woodland led in the Middle Ages to sophisticated systems of management so that what remained could be as productive as possible for timber, coppice wood, pasture and game.

Beryl Schumer's *Wychwood* is an important contribution to this new phase in the writing of woodland history. When first published it put forward the novel view that much of the wooded area of Wychwood at the beginning of the Anglo-Saxon period had once, in prehistory, been cleared land; in other words it introduces a concept of cycles of clearance and regeneration which has now been accepted for other similar areas, as in Christopher Dyer's *Hanbury: Settlement and Society in a Woodland Landscape* (1991), another Leicester Occasional Paper. Also novel is her conclusion that there was a very real limit to woodland clearance in Wychwood, a limit set by the need to conserve the woodland resources whose management she describes. Moreover, this book contains a great deal of detail for the people of Charlbury and of the surrounding Wychwood countryside, with many insights into the origins and early history of their own particular places. They are privileged to have this important book, now republished, about their region, just as I feel privileged to help the new launch in a small way by contributing this Foreword.

Department of English Local History,
University of Leicester.

Notes

1   *Times* obituary of Professor H. P. R. Finberg; M. Beresford in a review in *Agricultural History Review* 41 (1993), 197.

2   The word 'tamed' appears on p.35 of the first edition of *The Making of the English Landscape* (1955). Later Hoskins wrote the following. 'I myself in my first book fell into the trap, or rather accepted the current doctrine, that until the Old English Conquest most of this country was uncleared woodland or undrained marsh or in many parts primeval moorland... We now need a completely fresh study of the distribution of woodland by, say, Romano-British times': 'Editor's introduction', in L. M. Munby, *The Hertfordshire Landscape* (1977), 22-3.

3   H. C. Darby, 'The changing English landscape', *Geographical Journal*, 117 (1951), 377-94. See also H. C. Darby, 'The clearing of the woodland in Europe' in W. L. Thomas (ed.), *Man's Role in Changing the Face of the Earth* (1956), 183-216.

4   M. Bloch, *Les caractères originaux de l'histoire rurale française* (1931), 5-14.

5   J. Birrell, 'Peasant craftsmen in the medieval forest', *Agricultural History Review*, 17 (1979), 91-107.

6   A. Everitt, 'River and wold', *Journal of Historical Geography*, 3 (1977), 1-19.

7   Strong proponents of this view were C. S. and C. S. Orwin, *The Open Fields* (1938), 40.

Introduction

When Professor Hoskins wrote *The Making of the English Landscape* in 1955, he expressed current opinion in his statement that 'the great majority of the English settlers faced a virgin country of damp oak-ash forest' and, referring to the landscape at the time of Domesday Book, that 'England was still in an early colonial stage of development, and it is in the light of pioneers, frontiers and forests that we must look at the tremendous activity of the eight or nine generations between the making of Domesday Book and the coming of the Black Death, which put a decisive end to the first great wave of medieval colonization'.[1]

In the period which has elapsed since the publication of that book ideas regarding the early medieval landscape have changed markedly, as Professor Hoskins himself pointed out in 1976.[2] Archaeological evidence has made it plain that large areas of England were cleared, settled and divided into field systems or pastoral 'ranches' as early as the Bronze Age,[3] while studies of the Saxon period based on charter evidence suggest that much of the land was as fully exploited early in that period as it was at the time of the Conquest.[4] The likely date of the most active destruction of the primeval woodland has now been pushed back from the Saxo-Norman period to the later Iron Age or Roman period,[5] while archaeological evidence suggests that some at least of the woodland of the medieval period was secondary, in that it covered prehistoric or Roman settlement sites.[6]

Ideas regarding the role of woodland have also changed, and it is now recognized that in the early medieval period this was not an unwanted remnant of primeval 'wildwood', useful only when cleared, but rather a carefully husbanded asset, subject to jealously guarded rights held not only by vills within or adjacent to the woodland, but by others sometimes many miles distant from it.[7]

The site and extent of the medieval woodland is now thought to have been determined not solely by physical factors such as soil type and terrain, but by a combination of these with political and economic factors, possibly of some antiquity, and varying in different parts of the country. The reconstruction of the Domesday woodland and information regarding its relationship to the surrounding region consequently become matters of historical interest, both as contributing to our knowledge of early communities and, especially, in providing an accurate picture of the amount of post-Conquest expansion and colonization.

This book attempts to reconstruct from documentary sources the Domesday woodland of the Wychwood region of Oxfordshire, an area which is both small enough to make possible the accurate location of the woodland in the landscape, and large enough to provide some variation in the history of land use within the region, and to act as a reasonable basis for comparison with other woodland areas. The region is also well, though unevenly, covered as regards source material for such a study. The primary source is of course Domesday Book, and fortunately in Oxfordshire the woods are described in terms of length and breadth and so are easily visualized in relation to the modern landscape. In this part of Oxfordshire, too, the Domesday entries can be compared with the information provided by the Hundred Rolls of 1279. These do not give any dimensions for the manorial woods, but they are recorded, as also is any assart land and the holdings of free and customary land, so that large-scale alterations in land use between 1086 and 1279 can be detected.

Wychwood was a royal Forest until 1857, so that there are numerous Forest records, the most useful being the maps and documents relating to the Disafforestation in the mid-nineteenth century, a Survey of 1609, and the Perambulation of 1300. The disafforestation documents provide a detailed picture both of the royal Forest of that date, and of the adjoining land which formed the Purlieus of the Forest.[8] The 1609 Survey describes the same area but also much additional land, and while some of this corresponds to the areas which were retained within the Forest by the Perambulation of 1300, the remainder consists of part, only, of manors which were placed outside the Forest at that date. The Survey appears to be related to an attempt by James I to obtain increased revenue from the Forests by farming out the right to collect assart rents,[9] and it seems logical to suppose that the area within the disafforested manors represents the area which was on record as having been wooded, and thus actually or potentially assart land. Such a suggestion must of course be supported by independent evidence wherever possible. The 1300 Perambulation is invaluable in that it describes the boundary between the areas which remained within the Forest and the woods which were being disafforested, so providing numerous details regarding the topography and ownership of the woods at that date.[10] Further information about the landscape of the Forest is given by references to wood or assarts in royal or manorial documents, and these must eventually be linked to the earliest accurate maps. In most cases these accompany Tithe and Inclosure Awards, although a few early estate maps exist, and the degree to which maps and documents can be correlated depends principally on the survival of field- and place-names.

Administrative units of the Wychwood region

County/hundred	Domesday manor	Medieval parish
Gloucestershire	Widford	Widford
Oxfordshire		
Bampton	Asthall	Asthall
	Witney	Witney
Banbury	(Charlbury)	Charlbury
Chadlington	Ascott d'Oyley)	Ascott
	Ascott Earl)	
	Chadlington (2)	unidentified
	Enstone	Enstone
	Fulbrook	Burford
	Milton (2)	Shipton
	Minster)	Minster
	Little Minster)	
	Over Kiddington	Asterleigh
	Radford	Enstone
	Sarsden	Sarsden, Charlbury
	Shipton (3)	Shipton
	Spelsbury	Spelsbury
	Stockley	Shipton
	Swinbrook - Shipton	Swinbrook
	Taynton	Taynton
Wootton	Bladon	Bladon
	Cogges	Cogges
	Combe	Combe
	Eynsham	Eynsham
	Glympton	Glympton
	Hanborough	Hanborough
	Nether Kiddington	Kiddington
	North Leigh	North Leigh
	Piriho	Eynsham, Stanton ?
	Stanton	Stanton
	Stonesfield	Stonesfield
	Woodleys	Wootton
	Wootton (2)	Wootton
	Wilcote	Wilcote
	Kidlington (detached)	(now North Leigh)

Also a detached portion of Bloxham (Bloxham hundred) now in Spelsbury parish.

1

The Wychwood Region

For the purposes of this book, the Wychwood region will be defined as the part of Oxfordshire which was within the Forest of Wychwood in the thirteenth century, that is, the area bounded by the Glyme, the lower course of the Evenlode, the Thames, the Windrush, the county boundary, and the Sarsbrook.[1] This was not the greatest extent of the Forest (it was considerably enlarged by Henry II and reduced to its earlier bounds after 1219), but it seems likely that it also represents the Forest of 1086, and it includes the great majority of the vills with rights and interests in the woodland which lay within the Forest. However, some vills to the east of the Glyme — Bladon, Hordley and Hensington — also appear in the Forest records and so must be included in the Wychwood region.

It must be emphasised that the area of the legal Forest — that is, the area whose inhabitants were subject to the Forest Law — was never at any date identical to the area covered by woodland. The boundaries of a Forest could change at the will of the king, and in the early part of the thirteenth century the boundaries of Wychwood Forest extended far beyond its woodland and included many manors for which no woods are recorded in Domesday Book. After the alteration of the boundaries in 1219, most of the manors remaining within the Forest had had woods recorded, but the Domesday entries show that they also had a great deal of arable land. Later, many woods were declared to be outside the Forest, but this did not necessarily imply that there was much alteration in the actual amount of woodland.

This area which will be studied covers a large part of the modern administrative district of West Oxfordshire, and formerly included parts of four hundreds, Chadlington, Wootton, Bampton and Banbury. It includes 28 medieval parishes and at least 40 Domesday manors, these varying in size and importance from the 33-hide royal manor of Shipton and the Bishop of Winchester's 30-hide manor of Witney, to one-hide manors such as Stonesfield and Wilcote held by minor lords.

The region lies at the eastern limit of the Cotswolds, and the land varies in height from over 700ft (213m) in the north-west, near Chipping Norton, to about 200ft (60m) in the Thames valley, in the south-east. It is cut by the valleys of three main streams, the Windrush, Evenlode and Glyme, which flow in a generally south easterly direction to join the Thames, although the Evenlode, in particular, has several changes of direction.

The geological strata in the region also tilt towards the south-east, but at a greater angle than the general slope of the land, producing geological differences across the region; and since the soil, in this area, is usually closely related to the geology, these differences directly affected land use and the siting of settlements.[2]

The main rocks are those of the Liassic and Oolitic series and Oxford Clay. The rocks of the Upper, Middle and Lower Lias occur in the Evenlode valley above Fawler, and are mostly clays (although at Fawler itself some ironstone appears); and these produce heavy soils, usually left in grass. Above these lie the rocks of the Oolitic series, Chipping Norton Limestone, Great Oolite, Forest Marble and Cornbrash, which produce loamy soils, fairly easy to work and very suitable for arable cultivation and for sheep grazing, as well as providing good building stone.[3] Surface water is scarce, however, and settlements are usually sited beside permanent streams, as at Shipton, or at the junction of the limestones and the Lias, where springs occur (for example, Chilson). The Oxford Clay, which overlies the limestones in the south-eastern half of the region, is heavier to work and is also often associated here with Glacial Drift which sours the soil, and in that case the land is used as pasture or woodland. Settlements on the

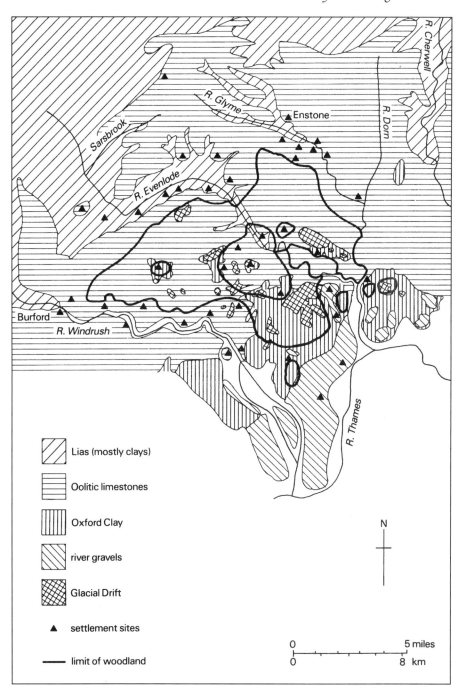

Map 1. The geology of the Wychwood region.

Clay and Drift, such as North Leigh, usually had to rely on ponds and wells for their water.

These geological and physiographical variations lead to three different types of settlement pattern. To the north and west of a line from Burford to Enstone the limestone ridges were formerly areas of open pasture, the Downs; the arable fields, also on the limestones, lay between the Downs and the springline; and below that were found the wetter pasture and the meadows, on the Lias and alluvium. To the south and east of that line the arable fields were situated in the valleys where the limestones occurred, while the higher ground, covered with Oxford Clay or Drift, was used as rough pasture or woodland. The villages were placed either beside the rivers or at the junction of the arable with the heath or woodland, and sometimes both types of settlement occur in the same parish, as at Asthall and Asthall Leigh. The third variation in the settlement pattern is provided by the villages in the Thames valley, Stanton and Eynsham, where the Oxford Clay occurs but is overlain by large areas of river gravels which are the site of both settlement and fields. Hanborough, in the lower Evenlode valley, presents a similar picture although the gravel terrace there is at a higher level, forming a T-shaped ridge on which the settlements of Church Hanborough and Long Hanborough are located.

2

Wychwood before 1086

The early history of the region has to be built up mainly from archaeological evidence, and since there has been no intensive and comprehensive field-walking, the amount of information available varies considerably. Nevertheless it implies a long history of occupation and use for both the 'arable' and the 'woodland' areas of 1086 as deduced in Chapter 3. (The term 'woodland' is here used for the area which was predominantly wooded, as opposed to the 'arable' areas where there were few trees and no woods.) Mesolithic flints found at Leafield and Fawler may indicate only the presence of nomadic hunters,[1] but settlement in the Neolithic period is indicated not only by crop marks on the Thames gravels but by several long barrows in, or at the edge of, the 'woodland'.[2] That at Ascott, in use between 3000 and 2000 BC, overlies evidence of Mesolithic and Neolithic occupation which implies a change from a woodland to a grassland environment.[3] Numerous round barrows, suggesting continued and expanding settlement during the Bronze Age, are found throughout the region, both in the cleared land and the 'woodland' of 1086, and the excavation of a settlement site dated to c.1700 BC at City Farm on the Eynsham-Hanborough boundary shows that it was in open grassland with wood nearby, an environment which does not differ greatly from that of the present day.[4]

The Iron Age saw the appearance in the landscape of several earthworks of considerable size, implying a large population. 'Camps' were constructed in Eynsham, Bladon and Lyneham, and excavation of the latter, dated to 200-100 BC, suggested that the surrounding area was already downland and grazed by sheep, as it continued to be for many centuries.[5] The largest Iron Age feature was Grim's Ditch, a discontinuous bank and ditch system, with associated features, which enclosed an area of 22 square miles. The northern part of it has been dated to the first century BC, and in places it was constructed over earlier settlement sites and ploughed fields. It has been suggested that the Ditch system formed an oppidum, although so far no main settlement site has been found.[6] It seems likely, however, that a small Iron Age farm existed at the site later occupied by the North Leigh villa,[7] while other Iron Age sites are known outside Grim's Ditch — in the Thames valley, and at Cogges, Asthall, Ascott, Chadlington and Kiddington.

Almost every parish has produced evidence of settlement in the Roman period, and this was particularly intense within Grim's Ditch, with eight known villa or farmhouse sites. Other indications of settlement are found along the Windrush at South Leigh, Cogges, Crawley, Minster, Asthall, Widford and Taynton; along the Evenlode at Charlbury, Chadlington, Chilson, Ascott and Kingham; along the Glyme in Wootton, Kiddington, Cleveley and Enstone; and in the woodland of western Wychwood. This relatively dense settlement pattern suggests that by the Roman period there was no large untouched area of primeval woodland left, although it does not imply that it had been cleared completely.

The archaeological evidence for Saxon settlement, however, shows a distinctly different pattern, in that the finds are restricted almost entirely to the area which later evidence suggests was cleared land in 1086, leaving the large area of Domesday woodland in which the period is at the moment represented only by two spear heads and one possible site near Brize's Lodge.[8] Later finds may alter this picture, but it seems clear that most of the villas and other Roman sites within the woodland were deserted.

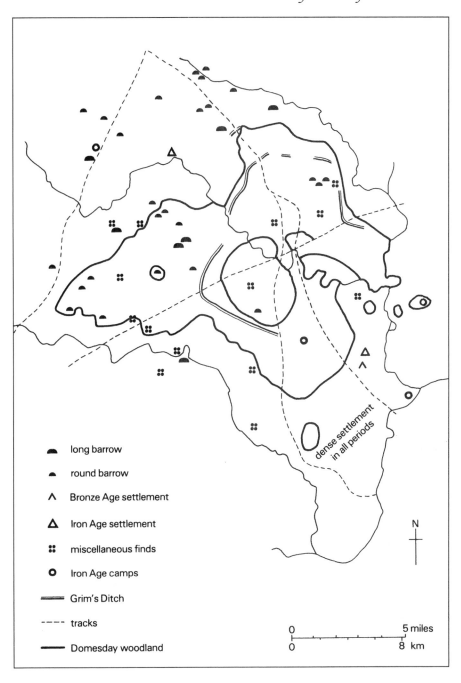

long barrow

round barrow

Bronze Age settlement

Iron Age settlement

miscellaneous finds

Iron Age camps

Grim's Ditch

tracks

Domesday woodland

dense settlement
in all periods

N

0   5 miles

0   8 km

Map 2. Pre-Roman Wychwood.

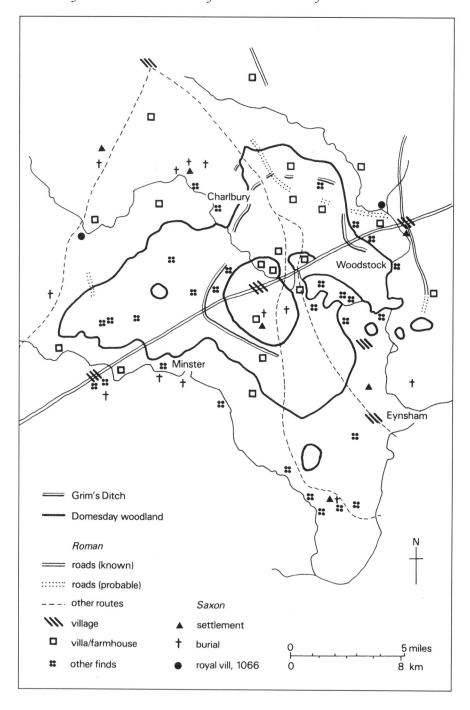

Map 3. The Roman and Saxon periods.

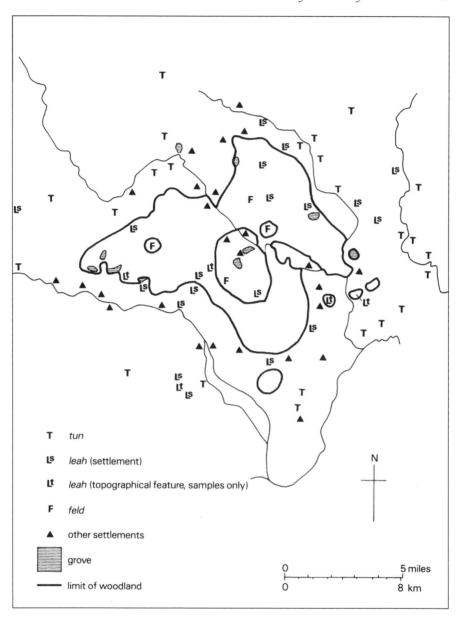

Map 4. Place-name elements in the Wychwood region.

The evidence from place-names

The same pattern appears on studying the place-names of the area, especially of those containing the elements *tun* and *leah*. It is now accepted that these elements differentiate between a settlement in an open, cleared environment, the *tun*, and one in a woodland setting, the *leah*, and in west Oxfordshire the two types of names occur in such close proximity that they almost define the Domesday woodland.[9] The *tun* settlements are found along the valleys of the Thames, Cherwell, Glyme, and to some extent the Windrush and the upper reaches of the Evenlode; and most of them were manors in 1086. The *leah* settlements form distinct clusters, one such consisting of Weaveley, Tackley and Hordley, between the Cherwell and the Glyme, where Tackley had a grove of wood in 1086. There is another (Barley Park, and the lost Eggesle and Puttesle) in Ducklington, which also had a Domesday wood,[10] and there is an isolated example at Tangley, in a still wooded valley to the north of Taynton. The majority of the *leah* settlements, however, occur in the area between the Glyme and the Thames-Windrush, within the circle of *tun* names, and this area also includes numerous examples where the element occurs in the name of a topographical feature, with no habitative significance (e.g., Pinsley Wood, Stockley Copse, and Gigley Green). The *leah* settlements were apparently of less importance than the *tuns* since only North Leigh is recorded in 1086; the others either remained as hamlets, or attained manorial or parochial status much later. The subsidiary nature of the *leahs* is shown by the fact that many manors included both a *leah* and another settlement bearing a *tun* or a topographical name under which the manor was recorded in 1086 (e.g., Stanton and South Leigh, Eynsham and Tilgarsley, Witney with both Hailey and Crawley); but although subsidiary, the *leah* was not necessarily a mere hamlet of landless cottagers, since many of these settlements had their own field systems.

One interesting feature of the Wychwood region is that many of the *tun* settlements also had a large amount of wood within their territory

(Chilson, Wootton, Kiddington and Glympton), but the *tun* seems always to have been separated from the wood by its arable fields, whereas the *leah* settlement was usually situated at the edge of, or within, the woodland or heath.[11]

Map 4 also shows occurrences of two other place-name elements, *feld* and grove. *Feld* is also found in association with woodland, but it implies a fairly large cleared area, and the element occurs in one Domesday manor (Stonesfield) and another settlement (Leafield) which is not recorded but was probably already in existence, as well as in other places (for example, Dustfield in Charlbury) where no settlements are known; but all of these occurrences are within the Domesday woodland. Grove, in this region, seems to have been used of a wood which was small and relatively isolated. The only one for which there is any evidence before 1086 is Fawsgrove, which lay at the edge of the woodland in the modern Swinbrook parish.[12] However Hensgrove, nearby, must be Swinbrook's Domesday wood, and it too is at the edge of the 'woodland', as are most of the other instances of the name, Priest Grove in Ascott, Gunnildegrove near Woodleys, and Lousie Grove and West Grove near Asthall Leigh; while some 'groves' were completely isolated (Holly Grove in Wilcote, Ordweygrove in Finstock, Hensigrove to the south-east of the Glyme — in Blenheim Park now — and Dean Grove in Dean). Thus the groves too help to define the woodland of the Saxon period.

Both archaeological and place-name evidence imply the presence of woodland in the Saxon period, and it seems that in the Wychwood region that period was not one of expansion, as is usually assumed, but of contraction of settlement, in that areas which had been occupied from the Bronze Age to the Roman period were apparently uninhabited and used only as wood-pasture.

3

The Woodland of 1086

For the last two hundred years of its life, the royal Forest of Wychwood consisted entirely of coppices and 'open forest' used as grazing by the deer and other animals, and the remnant which is called Wychwood today is also wooded. These facts may have reinforced the commonly held idea that woodland and forest are synonymous, but in the medieval period Forest was a legal term, relating to the preservation of the beasts of the chase, and a Forest did not necessarily have any woodland at all within its bounds. However, the confusion between the medieval and the modern meanings of the word persists, and since the (legal) Forest of Wychwood reached as far as the county boundary in the thirteenth century and a wood was recorded in the Domesday Book for Taynton which lies next to that boundary, it is often assumed that the woodland of Wychwood also extended as far as Gloucestershire. No attempt was made to prove this, since earlier writers on Wychwood were less interested in its topography than in the impact of the Forest Law on the people of the region and the activities of the medieval Foresters and the members of the gentry and aristocracy who held the same position in later centuries.

However, the woodland of Wychwood was not as extensive as is often believed, and in this chapter the evidence for early woodland is discussed in an attempt to gain as exact a picture as possible of where it was, and what it was like.

Another misconception about medieval Forests is that the woodland in them belonged entirely to the king. There was usually a core of royal woodland, but the rest of the woods belonged to manors held by other lords.

The earliest comprehensive evidence about the woodland of the Wychwood region is given in Domesday Book, and the entries there are summarised in map 5 and table 2. Each of the woods recorded there will be discussed, to build up a complete picture of the landscape of the region.

Table 2 also shows the references to woods in the Hundred Rolls and the Wychwood Perambulation of 1300. The entries in the Hundred Rolls are particularly helpful in that it is usually stated whether the woods are 'in the covert [continuous woodland] of Wychwood', while the boundary points in the Perambulation help to fix the location of many of them. Throughout this chapter, numbers in parentheses refer to woodland belonging to the manors listed in table 2 and shown in map 5. The woods which belong to the Crown are discussed first, then those that have been proved to be detached from their manorial centre, and the remainder are grouped topographically.

The woods of Domesday

Domesday Book poses some problems in that the woods belonging to the royal manors of Shipton and Wootton were merely said to be 'within the King's Inclosure' with no size stated, while it is not immediately clear what the entry regarding the three demesne Forests of **Woodstock**, **Cornbury** and **Wychwood** means in terms of actual woodland.[1] However, it seems certain that this woodland which belonged directly to the king, and was not attached to any manor, can only have consisted of a somewhat smaller Woodstock (Blenheim) Park, the park at Cornbury, and the area of woodland which remained in royal hands until the nineteenth century. These all have a continuous history of royal ownership and use as wood or wood pasture throughout the medieval period, and apart possibly from a small assart at Leafield there is no evidence that this demesne woodland was ever reduced in extent.[2]

	Manor	1086	1279	1300
1	Ascott	3 × 2f	in Wychwood	o
2	Asthall	13 × 10f	Asthall Wood	o
3	Bladon	1 × ½1	in regard of Wychwood	
4	Bloxham	13½ × 9f	no record	*
5	Charlbury	—	in Wychwood	o
6	Cogges	18 × 6f	in Wychwood	o
7	Combe	1½ × 1½l	in Wychwood	*
8	Cornbury	Demesne	—	*
9	Ducklington	3 × 2f	park	
		3 × 2f		
10	Enstone	11 × ½l 4f	in Wychwood	o
11	Eynsham	1½l × 11 2f	in regard of Wychwood	o
12	Fulbrook	6 × 2f	in Wychwood	
13	Glympton	6 × 6f	in Wychwood	o
	The Frith	—	in Wychwood	o
14	Hanborough	7 × 7f		*
15	Hordley	—	in Wychwood	*
	Kiddington			
16	Nether	5 × 1f	in Wychwood)	
17	Over	11 × 3f	in Wychwood)	o
18	Kidlington	3 × 3f	—	o
19	Minster	11 × 4f	in Wychwood	o
20	Milton	11 × 4f	—	—
21	North Leigh	1½l × 11	out of regard	o/*
22	Sarsden	11 × 7f	in Wychwood	o
23	Shipton	Inclosure	in Wychwood	o
24	Spelsbury	11 1f × 7f	in Wychwood, out of regard	o
25	Stanton	11 × ½l	in Wychwood	o
26	Stonesfield	5 × 2f		*
27	Swinbrook	3 × 1f		o
28	Taynton	11 × 4r	in Wychwood	o
29	Wilcote	4 × 1f	—	o
30	Witney	3 × 21	free chase	*
31	Woodstock	Demesne		*
32	Wootton	Inclosure		*
33	Wychwood	Demesne		*

f   furlong
1   league

o   within Wychwood Forest before 1300 Perambulation
*   within the bounds of the 1300 Perambulation

Demesne   demesne forests, 1086
Inclosure   'within the King's Inclosure'

Domesday *grava* and spinneys omitted.

Table 2. Domesday woodland of west and north Oxfordshire.

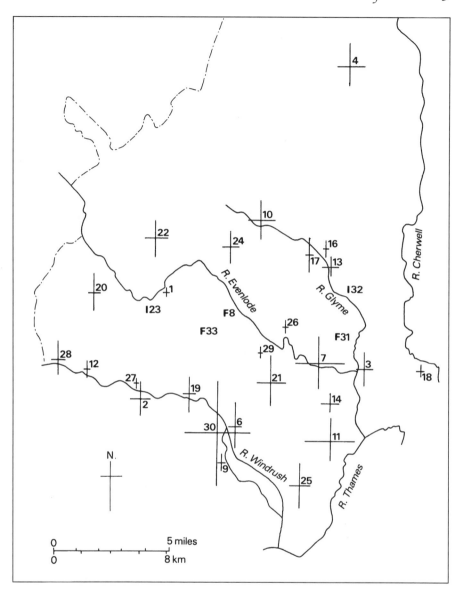

Map 5. Domesday woodland. Numbers refer to manors listed in Table 2, opposite. Nos. 5 and 15 do not appear, since the woodland belonging to Charlbury and Hordley was not recorded in Domesday Book. **F** indicates the three royal demesne forests (Woodstock, Cornbury and Wychwood).; **I** indicates the woods belonging to Shipton and Wootton manors, which were merely said to be 'within the King's Inclosure', with no dimension stated.

As for the royal manors, **Wootton**'s wood (32) is recorded in a charter of AD 958, although unfortunately in an incomprehensible fashion; however, the oddly-shaped portion of Wootton parish which lies to the west of the Woodstock-Chipping Norton road was included in the Forest by the 1300 Perambulation and also described in the 1609 Survey, and the later woods and medieval assarts belonging to Wootton can all be located in that area.[3]

There is no evidence of any woodland within the area covered by the modern parish of **Shipton**, but the medieval manor was large, and included the hamlets of Ramsden and Leafield. By the thirteenth century Shipton was held by the de Clares, Earls of Gloucester, and Matilda, Countess of Gloucester, was responsible for the assarting of the wood of Hulwerk to provide additional arable for Ramsden; while a Survey in 1555 stated that four coppices, Rowbarowes, Ezeswell, Blakewell and Studley, which lay between Ramsden and Leafield, belonged to Shipton.[4] This evidence proves that Shipton's woodland (23) was actually to be found between Leafield and Ramsden, and was separated from Shipton itself by the royal demesne woodland and the hamlet of Langley.

This was by no means the only piece of detached woodland in the region. In 1857 a detached portion of **Taynton** parish was located within the Purlieus of Wychwood, and this same area was described as Taynton Woods in 1609. It also corresponds to the separate area of woodland described in the Taynton charter of 1059, and so is undoubtedly the wood recorded in Domesday Book (28).[5]

Other detached areas of woodland are those recorded in 1086 for Kidlington and Bloxham. The wood belonging to **Kidlington** manor (18) was given to Osney Abbey in 1216, when it was described as 'the wood called Coggeswoode formerly belonging to the vill of Kidelinton', and it can be identified as the area called 'Osney Wood als [alias] Osney Hill' in the 1609 Survey, which lies immediately to the north of Cogges Wood (in Cogges) and about five miles from the nearest part of Kidlington parish.[6] **Bloxham** Wood (4) was even further from the centre of the manor, for the 1300 Perambulation locates part of it in

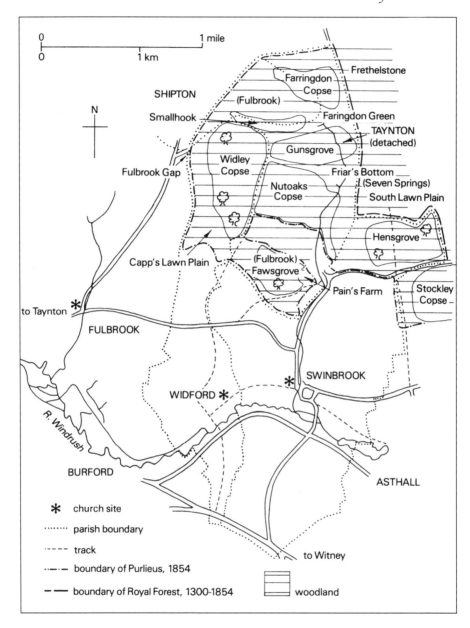

Map 6. Fulbrook, Widford, Swinbrook and Taynton parishes.

(Sources: Fulbrook Inclosure Award, 1818, 1819: Oxfordshire CRO, Bk 66; Fulbrook Tithe Award, 1851: PRO, IR29/27/62; Fulbrook, Shipton & Taynton Inclosure Award, 1861: Oxfordshire CRO, Bk 32; Swinbrook and Widford Inclosure Award, 1861: Oxfordshore CRO, Bk 32; Asthall and Swinbrook Estates, 1925: Bodl., GA Oxon. c. 238; W. Bryan Wood, Map of the Forest and Purlieus of Whichwood, 1854: PRO, MR 1682.)

the Ditchley area, in what is now the south-eastern part of Spelsbury parish, and another section, the wood of Amary de St Amand, in the northern part of Stonesfield parish.[7]

Some apparently outlying woods are those belonging to Fulbrook, Milton and Sarsden, and of these **Milton**'s is the least well documented, since it does not appear in any later records. In 1086 the woodland (20) belonged to the smaller, 1-hide manor in Milton, and in the thirteenth century that manor was held by the hereditary Forester of Wychwood.[8] It seems probable that Milton's wood was assarted to form part of the Forester's manor of Langley, for which there is no Domesday record, and this idea is supported by the fact that part of that manor is described in a sixteenth-century survey as 'Mylton and Langley'.[9] If it is correct, Milton's woodland too was detached from the rest of the manor, and adjacent to the royal woodland.

Three areas of woodland were recorded as belonging to **Fulbrook** in 1272, and in 1854 these were still within the Purlieus of the Forest.[10] One, consisting of Smallhook and Farringdon Copses and the intervening plain, formed an odd extension of Fulbrook parish linked to the rest by a very narrow neck of land at Fulbrook Gap. However the others were both detached, Fawsgrove separated from the village of Fulbrook by the manor of Widford (see map 6), while West Grove and Lousie Grove were even further away, near Asthall Leigh, and an adjoining part of Fulbrook's woodland had been assarted c.1306, eventually providing additional fields for Leafield. (It is possible that the hamlet of Field Assarts came into being as a result of this.) All of these areas may represent the Domesday woodland (12), although the dimensions do not support this, and it is possible that the woods near Asthall Leigh were added to Fulbrook in the twelfth century when Fulbrook and Asthall were held by the same lord.[11]

Parts of **Sarsden** are wooded today, and it might be thought that the Domesday woodland (22) was located within the parish. However, the Sarsden manor of 1086 was too large to consist merely of the modern parish, and in 1279 the descendant of the Domesday lord of Sarsden was overlord not only of Sarsden but also of part of Chadlington

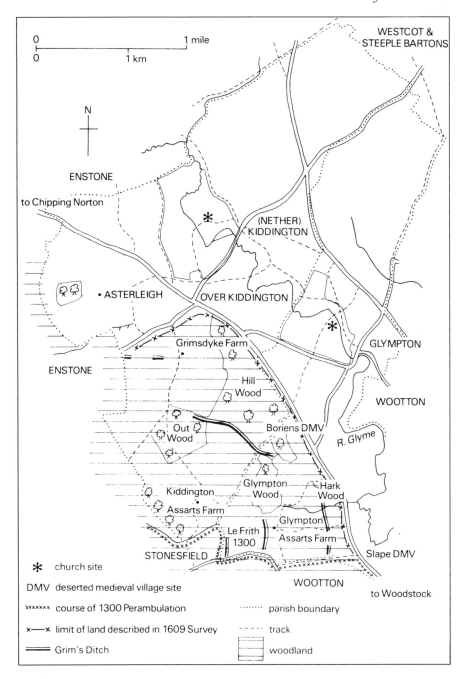

Map 7. Glympton, and Kiddington and Asterleigh.
(Sources: Herbert Barnett, *Glympton, the History of an Oxfordshire Manor*, Oxfordshire Record Society, V, 1923.)

(Chadlington Wahull) and of Pudlicote and Chilson, none of which were recorded in Domesday Book.[12] In 1279 the wood belonging to Sarsden was within the covert of Wychwood and the 1300 Perambulation makes it clear that the woods belonging to Sir John Golafre (of Sarsden) and the lord John FitzNigel (of Chadlington Wahull) were in Knighton Copse, adjacent to the royal woodland.[13] This was three miles away from the vill of Sarsden, but was described as 'parochia de Sarsden' in 1609,[14] and the area once occupied by the wood still forms a large rounded extension of Chilson. It too was within the Purlieus of the Forest in 1854, as were the woods of other manors in this part of the region — **Ascott** (1), **Widford**, **Swinbrook** (27), **Asthall** (2) and **Crawley** in Witney manor (30). In these cases the wood was within the manor and parish boundary, and adjacent to the royal woodland.

Minster's wood (19) was not within the Purlieus in 1854 since it had been disafforested in 1442, but the Tithe Award Map of 1830 shows 300 acres of wood still stretching across the northern part of the parish, while the names of adjoining fields, Pigrooting and Groves, suggest that these too may once have been woodland.[15]

For the whole of the western part of Wychwood there is very little evidence of assarting except in the woods belonging to Shipton and Fulbrook, and at Langley; and indeed the 10 ploughs recorded in 1086 for Ascott, and the 13 for Minster, for example, imply that the woodland cannot have been more extensive than has been deduced.[16] It is clear that there was in fact very little alteration in the amount of woodland here, so that the boundary of the Purlieus in 1854 should agree very closely with the woodland boundary of 1086. Since this also agrees with the area described in the 1609 Survey, it suggests that the Survey can be used as an indication of the extent of the Domesday woodland in the area north of the Evenlode where the documentation is much less complete, and where there was considerable assarting.

In some cases it is obvious that the Survey must describe the Domesday woodland. In the parishes of **Glympton** and **Kiddington** (see map 7) the Survey includes the land bounded on the north and east by the road from Woodstock to Enstone and the track from Over

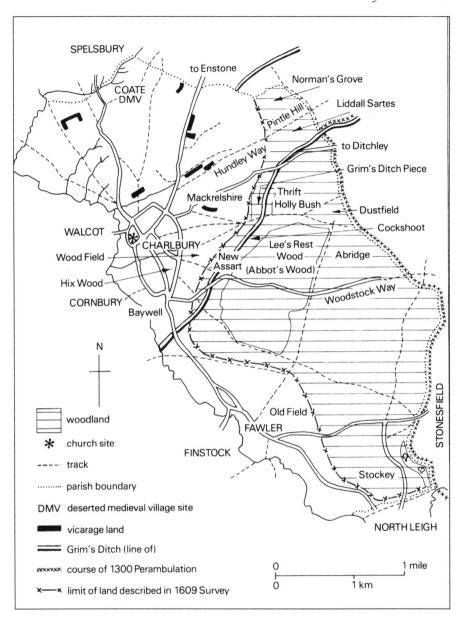

Map 8. Charlbury and Fawler.

(Sources: Charlbury Tithe Award: PRO, IR29/27/30, IR30/27/30; W. Bryan Wood, Map of the Forest and Purlieus of Whichwood, 1854: PRO, MR 1682.)

Kiddington to Ditchley,[17] an area which is separated from the rest of those parishes by a steep-sided valley and which even today contains several woods and farms which bear, or bore, assart names.

In **Charlbury**, however (see map 8), there are no such obvious changes in the terrain, the woodland has now disappeared, and the medieval assarts were added to the common field system so that there was no apparent difference between the original and the assart fields. Fortunately the Tithe Award map shows the location of a large number of the fields whose names are recorded in the 1609 Survey and in medieval references to assarts, and these are all found in the eastern and northern part of Charlbury, on the line of, and within, the suggested line of Grim's Ditch in that area.[18] The Tithe Award provides a further hint as to early land use there in the location of the strips belonging to the Glebe. These were presumably allocated at an early stage in the history of the parish, from fields existing at that time, and there is no evidence that they were added to when assarts were made. In Charlbury it is noticeable that the Vicarage strips were all in the west, and none in the area which, the Survey implies, was woodland.[19]

For **Fawler**, which was in Charlbury parish, the Tithe Award is not as helpful as it is for Charlbury, since it gives very few of the names recorded in earlier documents. However the area described in the 1609 survey was 986 acres, suggesting that at least half of that vill was wooded in 1086. Part of the woodland (Lee's Rest Wood) survived until the nineteenth century and medieval records of assarts at Stockey and elsewhere along the boundary with Stonesfield and Bloxham Wood indicate that this woodland was again in the north and east, with arable land beside the Evenlode.[20]

Enstone parish has a long tongue of land which lies between Kiddington and Glympton, on one side, and Spelsbury and Stonesfield on the other, and this is the area described in 1609.[21] Some woods survive, and all the references to assarts can be located here. Its north-ernmost part is Winchcombe Assarts, which was assarted in 1307, and the adjacent fields to the north belong to Radford which is recorded in Domesday Book but had no woodland, so that the boundary between woodland and arable is easy to determine in this area.[22]

Only in **Spelsbury** manor is there any evidence that the medieval woodland was more extensive than the area detailed in the 1609 Survey. That area was still almost completely wooded at that date (as it is today), but assarts in Spelsbury are recorded in the late thirteenth century, and in 1552 tenants in two of its hamlets, Taston and Fulwell, are recorded as paying rents for assart land. This presumably occupied the area between the two hamlets, probably extending as far as the surviving wood at Henley Knapp.[23]

It is apparent that, wherever additional evidence is available, it supports the theory that the 1609 Survey does indicate the extent of the Domesday woodland. However, in the case of those vills which were retained within the bounds of the Forest by the 1300 Perambulation the Survey is less helpful, because the whole of the vill is described, including the meadows, common fields, and even the house sites, and consequently analysis of this information and of any medieval references to wood and assarts is needed before the site of the Domesday woodland can be determined.

In **Stonesfield** this is easily done, since there was only 'land for 1 plough' in 1086, and the fields of that time probably consisted of Church Field (40 acres) and part of Home Field, immediately adjacent to the village. The rest of Home Field may have been wood then, and the area just north of the village, known as Gennett's Sarte in 1609, was still Gerner's Wode in 1300.[24]

The 1609 Survey showed that **Combe** had several common fields (West Field, Berry Field, Home Field and the two fields belonging to the hamlet of East End) which stretched along the Evenlode and probably correspond to the 5 ploughlands of 1086. But in the northern part of the parish there were assart fields (e.g. Wootton Sartes, Coome Old Sarte) which were separated from the rest by Combe Green, a long narrow area of pasture which extended from Woodstock Park to Notoaks Wood; and these fields were presumably the location of the Domesday woodland.[25]

In the case of **Hanborough**, the 1609 Survey (and later maps) showed three woods, Pinsley Wood, Mill Wood and Abel Wood, as well as a large area of heath; but it is probable that the northern part of the parish, which contained the heath, Mill Wood and Abel Wood, belonged in 1086 not to Hanborough, but to Stanton.[26] This leaves Pinsley Wood, in the centre of the parish, as the location of the Domesday woodland, with the addition of an adjacent field, The Assarts, since 28 acres of assart land is recorded for Hanborough in 1279 (see map 9).[27]

In **Hailey**, which with Crawley formed part of Witney manor, the 1609 Survey describes the two common fields and also a large number of closes of varying sizes.[28] The common fields must have been in existence in 1086, to provide sufficient arable for the 25 ploughs of Witney manor; but the large amount of woodland recorded in Domesday Book makes it certain that this must have covered the rest of Hailey as well as including the woods in the northern part of Crawley which survived until the nineteenth century.[29] This is confirmed by the many breach and assart field-names in Hailey, including 'the Bishop of Winchester's Assarts' which are recorded in 1609 and can be located immediately to the north of the common fields, and also by references in the Bishop's Pipe Rolls of the mid-thirteenth century to the woods of *Swaneye* (now the fields near Swanhill Farm) and of *Fermodshee*, said to be near Ramsden.[30]

The other manor which had Domesday woodland and is described in the 1609 Survey is **North Leigh**, but the Survey describes only part of the parish, corresponding to the area within the 1300 Perambulation, and it is not clear why this had been retained within the Forest at that date. The area includes the church (which has a Saxon tower) and the manor house site, as well as part of the early common fields, and is unlikely to represent the Domesday woodland.[31] Evidence for this is very scanty; assarts of unknown size and location were recorded in the late twelfth and thirteenth centuries, but the woods were freed from regard in 1251, so that there are no later entries in Forest documents. In 1279 the tenants held 75 acres of assart, but no record of separate assart land can be found in a manorial survey of 1581, the assarts presumably having been incorporated in the common field system of

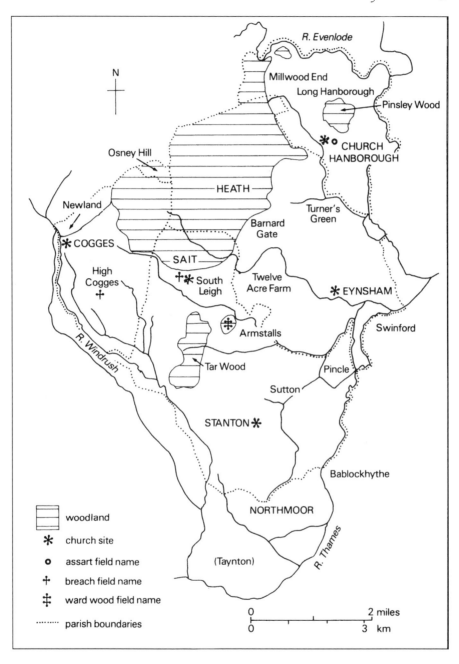

Map 9. South-east Wychwood ('the Forest of Piriho').

the manor.[32] The names of two of those fields, Over and Nether Riding, could be taken to indicate assarts, although every other example of a riding in this region refers to a track or road rather than an assarted area, and these fields lay on either side of the road from East End (North Leigh) to Ashford Bridge. Once again the evidence of the glebe land may differentiate between the early fields and the later assarts, and in North Leigh its evidence is supported by the location of the strips belonging to the tenement which is thought to represent the original demesne of the manor. In 1581 neither this holding nor those of the 'parson' or the vicar had any land in Nether Riding or Beyond the Bridge, and they had very few strips in Over Riding, for which there is independent evidence to show that it included some assart land.[33] It seems clear that North Leigh's Domesday woodland (21) occupied the eastern part of the manor, beside the Evenlode, but it may also have included the heath which stretched along the southern boundary until the Inclosure of the parish in 1759.[34]

The heaths in North Leigh and Hanborough were continuous with the wood and heath belonging to Cogges, Eynsham and South Leigh which are shown on maps of the eighteenth and nineteenth centuries. This area, however, was not included in the 1609 Survey,[35] and in trying to relate the recent landscape to that of 1086 one has to rely solely on medieval references to assarts and surviving field names. **Eynsham** had the largest wood, $1^1/_2$ leagues x 1 league 2 furlongs (11).[36] The abbot of Eynsham was occasionally fined or pardoned under Forest Pleas in the Pipe Rolls, but the only assarts which can be definitely assigned to Eynsham (as distinct from other manors held by the Abbey) are 'a purpresture containing 14 perches from the common pasture of Eynsham and Hanborough and an assart containing 15 acres' recorded in 1274, and another 1-acre assart.[37] In the first edition of this book these assarts were wrongly identified as a small enclave on the Heath, Parlo's Closes, but they are more likely to have been at Blowen (Cooks Corner); otherwise a map of 1769 shows a large area of wood and heath whose dimensions agree very well with a description of the bounds of Eynsham's woodland given in 1449 — which bounds, again, agree very well with those of the northern part of Eynsham recorded in a charter of 1005. Altogether there is nothing to suggest that Eynsham's Domesday woodland differed significantly from the 1482 acres of wood and heath recorded in the eighteenth century.[38]

This woodland was separated by a track from that belonging to **Cogges**, of which Cogges Wood still remains. It was formerly fringed on the west and south by a considerable area of heath, while a small group of 'breach' field-names to the south of High Cogges suggests earlier woodland in that area also, although there is no definite documentary evidence of assarting. In 1241 when the manor was sold to Walter de Grey, archbishop of York, it had been divided between two heiresses, and one moiety included 203 acres of wood.[39] Walter de Grey had the woods freed from regard, but the large amount of wood and heath surviving in the eighteenth century suggests that this did not lead to any change in land use within the manor.[40]

Stanton in 1086 included **South Leigh**, and presumably also the northern part of Hanborough.[41] It had a large wood, 1 league x $^1/_2$ league, and it is difficult to decide where this wood was. As stated above, there was wood and heath in the northern part of Hanborough, and there was also heath in the north of South Leigh, continuous with the heaths of Cogges and Eynsham, and also a wood, Tar Wood, in Stanton itself. By 1279 the land in Hanborough was recorded under that manor, but a manorial wood was still recorded under Stanton, and presumably this represents the Domesday wood. The heath in South Leigh was probably not large enough, and it seems likely that the Domesday woodland (25) was in the area where Tar Wood is still to be found, since this, with adjacent fields whose irregular boundaries suggest that they too were once woodland, remained as an almost detached part of Stanton within the more modern parish of South Leigh.[42] An additional area of woodland is implied by the field-names of Tar Ward Wood Piece, Hither Ward Wood Piece, and Long Ward Wood Piece, which were separated from Tar Wood by The Lawn, and which probably represent the wood held in 1279 by Henry de la Wade, lord of

Vill	Known or possible assarts			Total acreage
	12th cent.	13th cent.	14th cent.	
Ascott	*	—	—	—
Asthall	*	—	—	—
Cogges	F	—	—	—
Fulbrook	*	—	++	130
Minster	*	—	—	—
Swinbrook	*	—	—	—
Taynton	*	—	—	—
Walcote	*	—	—	—
Wilcote	—	?	—	—
Crawley		+	—	23
Eynsham	*	+	—	
Hanborough	—	+	—	
North Leigh	A	++	—	?500
Ramsden	?A	+++	—	200
Stanton	A	+	—	
Wootton	*	++	—	80
Charlbury	—	+	+++	330
Combe	*	+++	?	485
Enstone	*	++	+++	560
Fawler	*	+	+	730
Finstock	A	++	+	
Hailey	A	++++	?++	1,490
Kiddington	F	+	?	
Langley	?A	+	+	
Leafield	?	+	+	
Spelsbury	—	+	++	
Stonesfield	—	++	+	
Ditchley	—	—	+++	

*	small fine) in Forest Pleas
F	large fine)
A	assart recorded in Forest Pleas or manorial records, unspecified size
+	<50 acres assart
++	50–100 acres assart
+++	100–200 acres assart
++++	>200 acres assart

The vills have been divided into three groups on the basis of the date and amount of assarting: those with little or none; those where assarting apparently ceased by the end of the thirteenth century; and those with evidence of assarting during the fourteenth century. Acreage has been derived from the 1609 Survey or manorial records.

Table 3. Records of assarts in Wychwood.

Manor	Domesday Book			Hundred Rolls	
	Hides	Plough-lands	Ploughs	Hides	Additional land
Asthall	11	15	13	9	45 acres
Bladon	5	7	5	4½	—
Cogges	5	—	—	6+	—
Enstone	24	26	21	26	—
Eynsham	15½	18	18	17	—
Fulbrook	12	15	17	12	27 acres
Milton	5	5	3	5	—
Minster	7	10	13	9	—
'Sarsden'	20	28	28	24	—
Stanton	20	23	22	22½	—
Swinbrook	4½	3	2	5	17 acres
Taynton	10	15	21	12†	10½ acres
Wilcote	1	1½	1	1½	—
Lineham*	10	14	15	15+	—
Fifield*	5	7	7	8	—
Combe	1	4	5	4	?300 ac. assart
Hanborough	9	12	10	10	38 ac. assart
North Leigh	10	10	14	11+	75 ac. assart
Stonesfield	1	1	2	1½	45 ac. assart
Spelsbury	10	16	16	15	6 ac. assart
Witney	30	24	25	30½	650 ac. assart

* Vills in the vicinity, included as examples of those with no woodland available for assarting.

† In 1279 the land at La More (Northmoor), which was presumably included in the data for Taynton in 1086, was described only in acres (180 total).

Notes

1 Milton in 1279 included another 10 virgates which do not correspond to any manor recorded there in 1086.

2 'Sarsden' = Sarsden, Pudlicote, Chilson and Chadlington Wahull.

3 One hide of land 'in Stanton' was located at Hanborough. This has been omitted from the 1279 figures for both manors.

Table 4. Arable land, 1086 and 1279.

one of the manors into which Stanton was then divided.[43] Assarts in Stanton are recorded in the late twelfth century and in 1235, the latter probably being the $16^1/_2$ acres held by Richard de Harecourt in 1258.[44] These may have been taken out of the wood, but it seems likely that these assarts were made in the heathland, since there is in South Leigh a group of fields whose names include the word *sait*, presumably a local variant of sart or assart, and these were located next to the heath.[45] To the south of these are another group of closes whose names include the word *breach*, suggesting an earlier expansion on to the heath.

Two remaining Domesday woods are those of Bladon and Wilcote, neither of which is recorded in the 1609 Survey.[46] The dimensions given for **Wilcote**'s wood, 4 furlongs by 1 furlong, approximate to those of the surviving Holly Grove and Coneygar Copse, suggesting that the amount of woodland in that small manor has changed little since 1086.

There is wood in **Bladon** today, occupying a hill-top site similar to that of Pinsley Wood in the neighbouring parish of Hanborough, but this is post-medieval, and it seems almost certain that the Domesday wood (3) was situated on the further side of the Glyme, away from the village, and now lies within Blenheim Park. It is recorded as having been taken within the Park in 1576, but part of it may have been emparked earlier and be 'the King's park of Bladon' which is recorded

---

Map 10 (opposite). Location of the Domesday woodland of west and north Oxfordshire. Numbers indicate village sites, while arrows indicate the exact location of the manor's woodland.

1	Ascott	14	Hanborough	26	Stonesfield
2	Asthall	15	Hordley	27	Swinbrook
3	Bladon	16	Nether Kiddington	28	Taynton
4	Bloxham	17	Over Kiddington	29	Wilcote
5	Charlbury		(Asterleigh)	30	Witney
6	Cogges	18	Kidlington	31	Woodstock Park
7	Combe	19	Minster	32	Wootton
8	Cornbury	20	Milton	33	Wychwood (woodland
9	Ducklington	21	North Leigh		area, not a village site)
10	Enstone	22	Sarsden	34	Fawler
11	Eynsham	23	Shipton	35	Finstock
12	Fulbrook	24	Spelsbury	36	Widford (Glos.)
13	Glympton	25	Stanton		

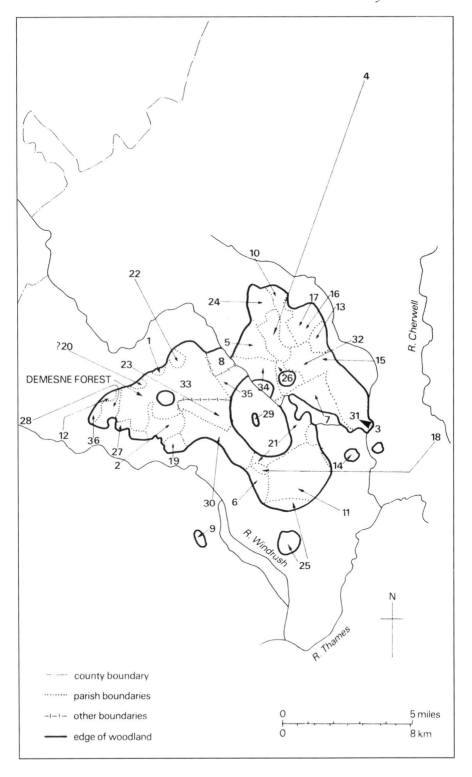

county boundary

parish boundaries

other boundaries

edge of woodland

in 1256.[47] In 1272 the king was to assart 'Bladen Wood in the Forest of Wychwood', but the wood was still recorded in 1279 as being in the regard of Wychwood Forest, and continued to be named as one of the woods of Woodstock manor, suggesting that the assart of 1272 may never have taken place.[48]

The hamlet of **Hordley**, which lies on the eastern bank of the Glyme, is not recorded in Domesday Book, but in 1279 its wood, Gunnildegrove, was said to be in the Forest of Wychwood, and a reference to it as a boundary point in the 1300 Perambulation locates it in the Woodleys area of Wootton, to the north of the wall of Woodstock Park as it then was.[49] The Park has been enlarged since that date,[50] and it is possible that the site of Gunnildegrove is also within the modern park wall.

All of the woods discussed so far either belonged directly to the king, or were manorial woods; but Wychwood also included two non-manorial, private woods, **Priest Grove** (in Ascott) and **Stockley Copse** (now in Asthall), which belonged to the rector of the church of Shipton and Swinbrook.[51] In the medieval period, however, there were no woods which belonged to individual lay owners.

The Domesday woodland has been discussed in detail to show that it is possible to decide its extent and location, in many cases with considerable accuracy. Some times, however, reliance has been placed on the existence or absence of evidence for assarting in the medieval period, and a true estimate of this is difficult to obtain. What little evidence there is for the period between 1086 and *c.*1250 consists only of references in isolated documents (usually cartularies) or of payments under Forest Pleas in the Pipe Rolls. The latter are not as useful as might be hoped since, in the earlier Rolls in particular, the records consist only of a list of the names of vills or persons with the amount of money due, and no indication of the offence. Assarting was only one of many actions punishable under the Forest Law. Later records give more details, with entries such as:

'Abbot of Eynsham 40/- for pigs agisted against the assize.'
'Vill of Combe 2 marks for waste in 2 regards.'

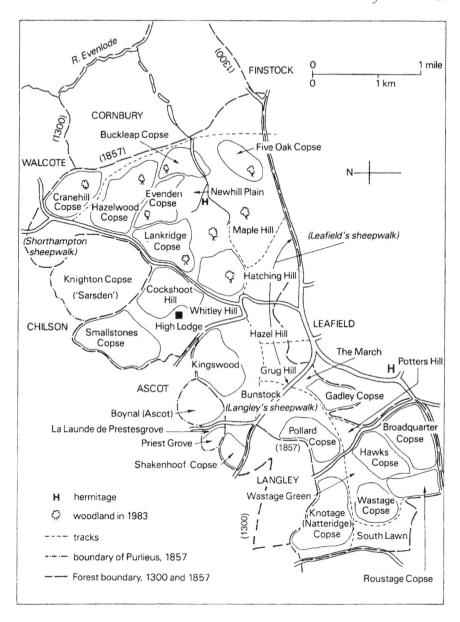

R. Evenlode

(1300)

FINSTOCK

0   1 mile
0   1 km

CORNBURY

Buckleap Copse

Five Oak Copse

(1300)

WALCOTE

(1857)

Newhill Plain

Cranehill
Copse   Hazelwood
Copse

Evenden
Copse

N

*(Shorthampton
sheepwalk)*

Lankridge
Copse

Maple Hill

(Leafield's sheepwalk)

Knighton Copse

('Sarsden')

Cockshoot
Hill

Hatching Hill

CHILSON

Smallstones
Copse

Whitley Hill

High Lodge

Hazel Hill

LEAFIELD

Kingswood

Grug Hill

The March

Potters Hill
H

ASCOT

Bunstock

(Langley's sheepwalk)

Gadley Copse

Boynal (Ascot)

La Launde de Prestesgrove

Priest Grove

Pollard
(1857) Copse

Broadquarter
Copse

Hawks
Copse

Shakenhoof Copse

LANGLEY

Wastage Green

(1300)

Wastage
Copse

H   hermitage

woodland in 1983

- - - -   tracks

Knotage
(Natteridge)
Copse

South Lawn

—·—·—   boundary of Purlieus, 1857

——   Forest boundary, 1300 and 1857

Roustage Copse

Map 11. The Royal Demesne woodland.

(Wychwood Forest, 1622-1857).

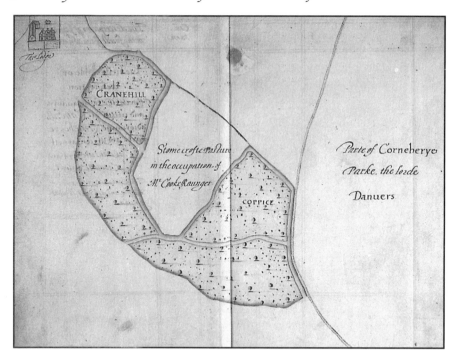

Cranehill Copse. This comes from *An Abstract of divers Manors landes and tenements graunted unto Prince Charles* (Charles I) *by our soveraigne Lord James his most loving father*, which includes a Survey of the coppices of Wychwood Forest made in 1617 by John Norden the elder and John Norden the younger. The Survey consists of a description of each coppice and an outline of its shape. For Cranehill it says that it 'conteyneth in Quantitie 74 ac, in Circuite 560 perches. This copice consisteth moste of thornes and is of about 16 years growthe'. The field within the copse was presumably cut out by one of the occupants of Ranger's Lodge, but the date of this encroachment is not known.

'Salomon de la Felde 1 mark for an offence against the vert.'
'Vill of Great Tew 100/- for concealing a stag which strayed in its fields.'

Such entries are more frequent than those recording assarts.[52] Sometimes, too, 'wastes and assarts and pleas of the Forest' occur in the accounts as a single item covering the whole county, with no information as to the people and places involved. The Forest Pleas of the late thirteenth and fourteenth centuries are more detailed, but some of those records have not survived.

The available evidence is summarized in table 3; some vills have been omitted for lack of evidence, and for others the only record consists of a payment in the Pipe Rolls, which was almost certainly not for assarts, since there is no other evidence for such. For those vills where the 1609 Survey indicates the presence of assarts there is generally some documentary evidence for these in the medieval period, although the acreage recorded usually falls short of the Survey figure, suggesting either the use of acres of different sizes or the loss of some documentation.[53]

It is sometimes assumed that a large amount of assarting took place in the period before 1184, when the Assize of Woodstock reinforced the administration of the Forest Law (a period for which there are very few records), and it is difficult to refute this except by attempting to relate the statistics for arable in 1086 with those of the Hundred Rolls. This can only be done if one assumes that the hides and virgates of 1279 can be compared with one or more of the hides, ploughlands, or ploughs recorded in 1086. It is generally agreed that the Domesday hide may not always be directly related to the area of land under cultivation (see, for example, the figures for Combe), but it has been suggested that the ploughland of 1086 does provide an estimate of the arable land, and can be compared with the hides and virgates of later surveys.[54] Table 4 shows the Domesday figures and also an estimate of the arable in 1279 in 'hides' which are calculated from the total number of hides, virgates and half-virgates recorded for those Wychwood manors which, it is reasonably certain, remained the same size throughout the period. The figures are crude, but, with the notable exception of Witney, the ploughlands of 1086 and the 'hides' of 1279 are in fairly close agreement, suggesting that there was not a large amount of unrecorded assarting.

The landscape of the Domesday woodland

It seems clear then that the extent of the Domesday woodland of the region can be decided with a reasonable degree of accuracy, and that it formed a relatively compact area stretching from the park at Woodstock to the Downs of Shipton and Fulbrook, and from Henley Knapp near Enstone to the heaths of South Leigh and Eynsham, with some isolated woods in Stanton and Hanborough (see map 10). However, this compact area was not uniformly and densely covered with trees, since it contained at least two large clearings in which were located the Domesday manors of Stonesfield, North Leigh and Wilcote; and these and other settlements in and around the woodland will be discussed in the following chapter.

Apart from these clearings there were probably other areas of relatively clear land between more densely wooded ones, and possibly these were natural in origin, since botanical evidence suggests that in places the vegetation would have been heath rather than wood.[55] The *Haethfeld* occurs in the bounds of the Eynsham charter of AD 1005, showing that Eynsham's woodland even at that date was similar to the mixture of wood and heath shown on eighteenth-century maps.[56] Maps of the same period depict the surviving part of the royal Forest as compartmented, with a pattern of coppices separated by large areas of open forest, lawns and wastes (see map 11).[57] The earliest description of these coppices occurs in a Survey of 1552, but fences around two of them are recorded as having been damaged by the passing of the queen's baggage train in the time of Edward III,[58] while their marked similarity in size and shape to the manorial woods (especially those around Knighton Copse and near Leafield) and the fact that their shape is in many cases determined by the dry valleys which separate them, suggest that they could be of much the same age as those woods. The 'open forest' between the coppices was to a large extent occupied by the sheepwalks of Langley and Leafield,[59] and since it seems unlikely that sheepwalk rights could have been acquired after the area had been placed under Forest Law, these sections may have been marked off for that purpose since the Saxon period at least.

The 1609 Survey shows that this division into areas of wood and of wood pasture occurred not only in the royal woodland but also in the smaller manorial woods. The main part of Fulbrook's woodland then consisted of Smallhook and Farringdon copses and 'one long narrow plain of pasture ground', and since the wood of Smelnoc was recorded in 1230, that arrangement cannot have been a recent development.[60] Another wood-pasture area for which there is early documentation is that belonging to Ascott which consisted of the wood of Boynal and a small pasture area called 'la launde de Prestesgrove' in 1300, which may represent the 4 acres of pasture recorded for the manor in 1086.[61] Similar separation into areas of wood and wood-pasture was found in Asthall and Crawley, although for these there is no evidence earlier than the 1609 Survey.[62]

The same organization probably existed to the north of the Evenlode. Some pasture areas, such as Callow Hill in Stonesfield, are shown on late maps, and the 1300 Perambulation provides hints as to the existence of others, in that it specifies the woods between which its course ran, but also includes boundary points whose names (Dustfeld, Bentleye and Poddeleye) suggest that they were clearings.[63]

Another feature of this part of the woodland is the grid of routes found there, visible today mostly as foot- and bridle-paths, and farm tracks. Many of them are recorded in the 1609 Survey, but only one in the medieval period, in 1300. This was then the mereway between Charlbury and Bloxham woods, but it was also the boundary of Banbury hundred, and is presumed to be a prehistoric trackway; while others of these tracks form parish boundaries, and must be of some antiquity.[64] For the rest of Wychwood, it is noticeable that the Saxon charters relating to the region all use 'ways' as boundaries in the wooded area; Taynton's wood was bounded by the Stony Way, the way to Fawsgrove, and the way to Widilea; Eynsham in its wooded section by the way to the boundary tree, the way to the Port Street, and the Port Street itself, while in the northern part of Witney manor the boundary points include Langley Way, the hunter's way, the green way, and the sheep way.[65] Other mereways between the royal woodland and the manorial woods are recorded in the 1300 Perambulation, and these must be of the same age as the woods themselves, that is, in existence before 1086 at least.

Much of the evidence for the nature of the woodland is late in date, and extrapolation back in time may not be valid; but it all tends to indicate that Wychwood in the medieval period was not an indeterminate trackless wilderness, but rather an organized area of wood and wood-pasture with definite and fairly stable boundaries, and clearly defined routes through it.

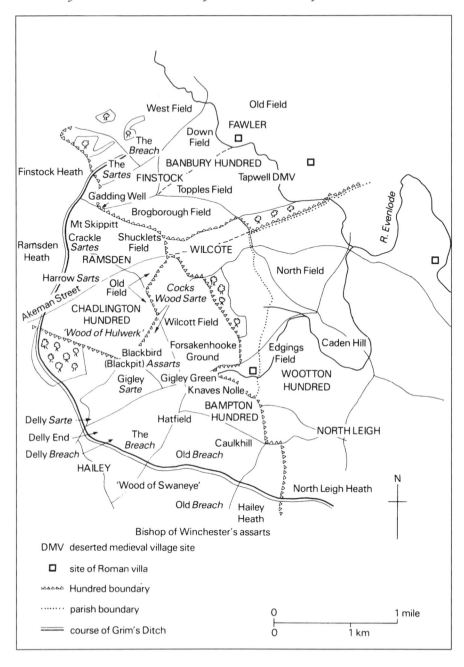

Map 12. The Wilcote area.

4

Settlements and Rights in the Domesday Woodland

The woodland depicted in the previous chapter differs in several respects from the earlier view of a large area of undeveloped 'wildwood' from which arose, after 1086, 'the new villages carved out of Wychwood which are the most tangible evidence of medieval expansion in the Oxfordshire landscape'. The villages specified in connection with this statement are Leafield, Ramsden, Fawler, Finstock, Hailey and Crawley, while other examples cited are Chilson, Asterleigh and South Leigh.[1]

The creation of these villages was inferred from the fact that they are not recorded in 1086, and appear in the records for the first time in the following two centuries, often in association with references to assarts. However, each of the vills mentioned above was part of a larger manor under whose name the Domesday entry was made, Leafield and Ramsden belonging to Shipton, Fawler and Finstock to Banbury, Hailey and Crawley to Witney, Chilson to Sarsden, South Leigh to Stanton, and Asterleigh to Over Kiddington, so that their omission from Domesday Book does not mean that the vills did not exist at that time.

In the case of **Leafield**, some evidence for its existence is found in the bounds of a charter for Witney manor, AD 1044. At the northernmost point, in what is now Crawley parish, the bounds include headlands, and since this part of Crawley was, and has remained, wooded, the fields to which the headlands belonged must have been cultivated from nearby Leafield.

An earlier charter for Witney (AD 969) suggests the presence of cleared, arable land in **Ramsden**, since the phrase *Ofling aecer* occurs at the point where the Witney boundary runs beside the Old Field of Ramsden.[2] Another clue is provided by the Domesday record for Shipton manor, which had a very large number of bordars (64, as against 54 villeins).[3] It seems likely that many of these were actually living at Ramsden, with others at Leafield, and that, although there was some arable land, they were engaged primarily in pastoral activity, as suggested by other field-names there: Swinepits, Lamber Leys, Hoggis Hay, and Cow Pasture.[4]

Ramsden lies next to **Wilcote**, which was a manor in 1086, and it is almost certain that the clearing in which Wilcote and **North Leigh** were located did not stop at their manorial boundaries, but spread into the adjoining manors. The known assarts in Ramsden, and the heath and wood which survived there until the nineteenth century, are all some distance from the Wilcote boundary, while in **Hailey** the surviving wood and the fields with assart or breach names are separated from the Wilcote and North Leigh boundaries by large groups of fields whose names have no woodland connotation (Caulkhill, Navelands, Forsakenhooke).[5] An additional piece of evidence for an extension of the clearing into Hailey is given by the description in 1347 of a piece of assart in Witney manor as 'in North Leigh on Caldehull', where North Leigh cannot refer to the manor of that name, but probably had its more general meaning of north clearing.[6] This part of Hailey was probably not cultivated in 1086; it was more likely to have been a heathy pasture such as still survived to a small extent until the nine-teenth century.

The clearing may also have extended into **Finstock**, and here the earliest record, c.1120, refers to a virgate and so implies arable land.[7] Some assarts are recorded there, at 'the chase of Gattwell' (Gadding Well), Lurteden and Paches Diche, but again most of these are situated at a distance from the Wilcote boundary, and it seems almost certain that Finstock too was already in existence in 1086.[8]

This large clearing, containing North Leigh, Wilcote, Ramsden, Finstock, and the northern part of Hailey, is of some interest, since it was bounded on the west and south by Grim's Ditch, and was the site of relatively dense occupation during the Roman period, with a village extending along Akeman Street between Wilcote and Ramsden, a villa at Shakenoak, and sundry finds at Mount Skippitt, Finstock and North Leigh which suggest additional settlements there. Continuity of occupation into the Saxon period has been postulated by the excavators of the Shakenoak villa,[9] and it is perhaps significant that the clearing was divided more or less evenly between four hundreds, since Hailey was in Bampton, Ramsden in Chadlington, Finstock in Banbury, and Wilcote and North Leigh in Wootton hundred.

On the other bank of the Evenlode from Finstock lay **Fawler**, and both were presumably included in the manor of Banbury and so were not recorded by name in Domesday Book. However, if the 1609 Survey accurately describes the Domesday woodland, it implies that the area of Fawler near the river was already cleared and settled in 1086. The earliest documentary records, in the thirteenth century, suggest a reasonably well-developed estate, because it had been divided between three of the bishop of Lincoln's knights, all of whom held a hide or more, to a total of 5 hides.[10]

The evidence for the location of the Domesday woodland, and the statistics for ploughland recorded in 1086, also imply that several other unrecorded settlements already existed. The customary land of **Hailey** and **Crawley** must have formed part of the land for 24 ploughs recorded in Domesday Book for Witney manor, and there were presumably hamlets where the men who worked those fields lived.[11] The same probably applied to the hamlets of **Sarsden** manor, where 28 ploughs were at work,[12] and for **Chilson** which, with Sarsden's woodland, lay on the other side of the Evenlode from the rest of the manor, this idea is supported by the absence of evidence for any significant alteration in the size of that wood. There was a Roman villa in Chilson, very close to the present hamlet, and it seems possible that the land there had been cleared and used for many centuries before 1086.[13]

Asterleigh formed one manor with **Over Kiddington**, and this was recorded as Chidintone in 1086, as Esterle and Cudinton in 1279, and as the manor of Asterleigh with the hamlet of Over Cudinton in 1302.[14] If Asterleigh was a secondary, post-Conquest creation it must have grown in importance very rapidly, since it was the site of the church and gave its name both to the late medieval manor and to the parish.[15]

South Leigh is not recorded before the late twelfth century, but one of these references is to the escheat of an estate worth £8, and this is unlikely to be a newly-created forest hamlet.[16] The other reference is to two virgates of land there, one from the demesne and one from 'the land of the men of Leya', which were given to Reading Abbey before 1176 together with an existing chapel, this again suggesting a fully developed estate; while in the Hundred Rolls there is nothing to suggest that South Leigh differed in any way from the other parts of Stanton manor. Whether in South Leigh, Sutton or Stanton itself the land was in virgates or half-virgates, held either of Richard de Harecourt or Henry de la Wade, and the same amount was paid for it.[17]

Another hamlet which has been thought to be of post-Conquest origin is **High Cogges**, and there is no documentary evidence to refute this since the Domesday record for Cogges is defective (no villein land being recorded).[18] However, the place-name itself, which means hills, is more suited to the site at High Cogges than to the riverside site where the manor house and the church were located.[19]

Forest hamlets and hermitages

It seems likely that all of these settlements were in existence before 1086, but there were others still smaller, whose date of origin it is impossible to determine. They were situated at the boundary between two or more manors, within or at the edge of the woodland, usually had no regular field system, and some were deserted in the late medieval period.

One of these is **Ditchley**, a small hamlet at the meeting-place of the woods belonging to Spelsbury, Enstone and Bloxham. The earliest references suggest that it was then the home of the keeper of Bloxham Wood, with extensions of the hamlet into Enstone and Spelsbury occurring later.[20] Other small hamlets north of the Evenlode were **Boriens** (Berrings) and **Slape**, Boriens being at the Glympton-Kiddington boundary, and Slape near the Glympton-Wootton boundary, and both at the woodland edge. These are recorded in the Hundred Rolls, and their inhabitants figure in the Forest records, but both sites are now deserted.[21]

In the south-western part of Wychwood was another hamlet, called **La Leye** in 1279, in which lived the tenants of both **Fulbrook** and **Taynton** manors whose land represents some, at least, of the odd acres recorded for those manors at that date. This seems to have been another hamlet devoted to the management of the woodland, since the Fulbrook tenants who held land there were Philip, son of Pagan de Mumbrey, who looked after 'the wood at La Leye', and John Palmere who kept the lord's pigs; while Taynton's tenant was Pagan who kept 'the wood towards La Leye' and was possibly the same man as Paganus de Stocleye who is recorded as being keeper of Taynton's woods. La Leye is probably an earlier name for Pain's Farm, which lies between the area once occupied by Taynton's detached woodland and Fawsgrove, which belonged to Fulbrook, and is close to the wood of Stockley. It is also bounded on the east and west by Swinbrook's wood, Hensgrove, and Widford's wood, Widley Copse, of which Richard son of Pagan was woodward in 1256 (see map 6). Pain's Farm presumably takes its name from this Pagan or an ancestor of the same name, which would suggest a thirteenth-century (or twelfth-century) origin for the hamlet; but if it was also known as La Leye it could have originated at an earlier date.[22] The presence of a round barrow beside the farm suggests the possibility of a long history of occupation.

Also within Taynton Woods there was a site described in 1609 as a 'decayed grange of Deerhurst Priory' and probably represented today by earthworks near Seven Springs, but this was presumably of post-Conquest origin, as also probably were the three hermitages in Wychwood, at Pheleley (in Bloxham Wood), Lovebury, near Leafield, and Newelme, within the royal woodland.[23]

In conclusion, it can be argued that the vills which were thought to be the result of post-Conquest assarting were already in existence in 1086, as also possibly were even smaller hamlets, and although some of these may have grown in size, it is hard to detect any completely new settlements within the woodland, with the possible exceptions of the Forester's 'manor' of **Langley** and the hamlet of **Field Assarts**. The evidence is in many cases circumstantial, but Domesday Book's deficiencies as an accurate indication of the number of settlements are now recognized, and perhaps 'the onus of proof rests on those who wish to claim that settlements were created after the Domesday enquiry'.[24]

Woodland rights

In the same way as the boundaries within the woodland were demarcated by 1086, and the settlements established, it seems likely that rights within the woodland were also fixed by that time, although all of the evidence for these is of much later date.

There were three principal woodland rights, apart from the ultimate right to cut it down and convert the land to arable, and these were the right to hunt game, the right to cut timber and underwood, and the right to graze animals there.

In a royal Forest, the right to hunt game, or more particularly the Beasts of the Chase (deer and wild boar), in both the royal and the manorial woods was the prerogative of the king and of those to whom he granted the privilege or responsibility. In Wychwood, however, the two towns of Burford and Witney had, by tradition, the right to hunt deer in the Forest on Whit Monday. There are no medieval records of this custom, but the ritual associated with the Hunts, involving the election of a Whitsun Lord and Lady and the calling together of the villagers by the blowing of 'peeling horns' made from curled strips of bark, suggest an early origin. Villagers from Bampton, Brize Norton and Ducklington were entitled to join in the Witney Hunt, and these two hunts seem to have been the only occasion on which vills situated wholly to the south of the Windrush had any connection with the Forest.[25]

The right to timber and underwood was less restricted in that the lord could take from his manorial wood whatever was needed for the upkeep of his manor, although unless special licence was obtained this could be done only under the supervision of the Forester, and excessive cutting, or 'waste', was punished by the temporary, or even permanent, confiscation of the wood. Accusations of waste were made regarding almost every wood in the Wychwood region at one time or another, and four of Fulbrook's woods were confiscated temporarily c.1300, while that part of Bloxham Wood which belonged to Amary de St Amand was confiscated and remained in the king's hands.[26]

A certain amount of wood (usually dead wood) could be taken from the Forest by vills outside the region, on payment of a fee to the Forester, and the Hundred Rolls record such payments by the vills of Duntrop, Little Tew, Dornford and Whitehill, and Hensington.[27] Tenants in Hordley, however, were responsible for the upkeep of Stratford Bridge, where Akeman Street crossed the Glyme, and they were entitled to take timber (fully grown trees) from the Forest for this purpose.[28]

The rights of common, however, provide the most interesting information about the use of woodland by the vills of the region. The pasture of Cornbury, and probably of Woodstock also, was reserved for the king's use,[29] but otherwise the pasture in both royal and private woods was shared by the tenants of many manors, and for this purpose the woodland seems to have been divided into two parts, each intercommoned by a different group of vills.

Common rights lasted longest in western Wychwood. In 1792 tenants in Ascott d'Oyley, Chilson, Pudlicote, Shorthampton, Walcot, Finstock, Ramsden, Leafield, Langley, Asthall, Asthall Leigh, Minster, Swinbrook, Fulbrook, Pain's Farm and Widford were recorded as having the right of common pasture in the royal woodland, while nineteenth-century maps show several of the privately owned areas as 'common to forest stock'.[30]

Evidence is less complete for the eastern part of Wychwood and there the pattern of common rights has to be built up from scattered references. In 1545 the free and customary tenants of the royal manor of Woodstock and its Seven Demesnes (Bladon, Hanborough, Combe, Stonesfield, Wootton, Hordley and Woodstock), as well as using the 'common or waste grounds of the manor and its members', could common their cattle in the 'common grounds and Michaelmas grounds' of Eynsham; and all the tenants and inhabitants had common on all the assart grounds in Fawler, Charlbury, North Leigh, Ditchley, Kiddington and Glympton, and also in all the commons and fields of North Leigh and South Leigh.[31] In practice the right of common in Eynsham seem to have been restricted to Hanborough, and that in North Leigh to Combe and Stonesfield; but in the Hundred Rolls Hordley claimed to have the right to pasture within the whole Forest.[32]

The non-royal vills had similar rights, as is shown by the statement in the Hundred Rolls that Combe Wood was common pasture for the whole country, and by a protest by Stonesfield tenants in 1738, that men from Spelsbury, Glympton and Charlbury were still commoning in Stonesfield although the fields and commons in those vills had been enclosed so that the men of Stonesfield could not exercise their own right of common there.[33] In 1547 Glympton was said to have common

---

Map 13 (opposite). Rights in the woodland of Wychwood.

Numbers indicate village site, while arrows indicate where tenants held the right of common pasture. For convenience, the same key has been used as for maps 5 and 10, but where no information is available numbers have not been included on the map.

1 Ascott	14 Hanborough	26 Stonesfield	38 Bampton
2 Asthall	15 Hordley	27 Swinbrook	39 Brize Norton
3 Bladon	16 Nether Kiddington	28 Taynton	40 Burford
4 Bloxham	17 Over Kiddington	29 Wilcote	41 Chilson
5 Charlbury	(Asterleigh)	30 Witney	42 Langley
6 Cogges	18 Kidlington	31 Woodstock	43 Leafield
7 Combe	19 Minster	32 Wootton	44 Old Woodstock
8 Cornbury	20 Milton	33 Wychwood	45 Pain's Farm
9 Ducklington	21 North Leigh	34 Fawler	46 Pudlicote
10 Enstone	22 Sarsden	35 Finstock	47 Ramsden
11 Eynsham	23 Shipton	36 Widford	48 Shorthampton
12 Fulbrook	24 Spelsbury	(Glos.)	49 South Leigh
13 Glympton	25 Stanton	37 Asthall Leigh	50 Walcote

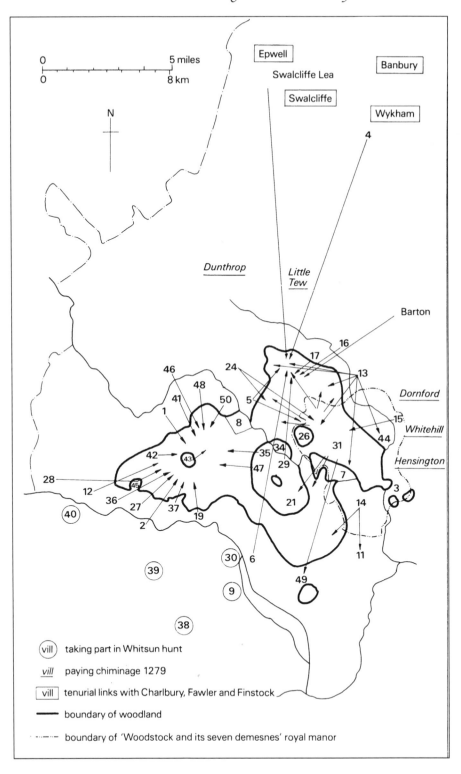

Epwell

Swalcliffe Lea

Banbury

Swalcliffe

Wykham

4

N

0 ___ 5 miles
0 ___ 8 km

Dunthrop

Little Tew

Barton

16

17

13

Dornford

46

24

5

15

Whitehill

48

41

50

8

26

31

44

1

Hensington

42

43

35 34

29

7

28

47

3

12

45

36

27

37

19

14

40

2

21

11

30 6

39

49

9

38

(vill) taking part in Whitsun hunt

vill paying chiminage 1279

vill tenurial links with Charlbury, Fawler and Finstock

━━━ boundary of woodland

·—·—·— boundary of 'Woodstock and its seven demesnes' royal manor rights for all cattle not only in Glympton and Stonesfield but also in Old Woodstock, Combe, Ditchley, Spelsbury and Kiddington, while further information about common rights is found in records of the early fourteenth century when disafforested areas north of the Evenlode were being assarted. Since the woods had been pastured in common, agreements had to be reached regarding the rights of the vills, and the abbot of Eynsham, as lord of Charlbury and Fawler, made such agreements with the earl of Warwick, lord of Spelsbury, and with Walter de Shobindun who may have farmed the demesne at Combe,[34] while the abbot of Winchcombe, as lord of Enstone, recorded agreements with Walter de Shobindun and with the lords of Asterleigh and Kiddington, Cogges, Barton, Bloxham, 'Wilcote' (an estate in Finstock and North Leigh), Spelsbury, and Swalcliffe La Lea.[35] The lord of Cogges also held Wilcote manor, and this agreement may refer to rights held by either vill, or both. Bloxham's right existed because of its own wood near Ditchley, and Barton's was presumably related to the wood at Sheer's Copse, which in 1609 belonged to Sesswell's Barton.[36] Swalcliffe La Lea however is not recorded elsewhere as having wood or common rights in Wychwood, but there were tenurial links between Swalcliffe and Fawler, and in 1086 both were probably part of the Bishop of Lincoln's Banbury estate. The bishop held the whole of Banbury hundred, of which Charlbury, Fawler and Finstock formed a detached part, and it has been suggested that they represent the woodland pertaining to the manors in the north of the county.[37] Charlbury was probably linked to Banbury itself, since it was held by the bishop until he granted it to Eynsham Abbey,[38] while Fawler and Finstock were sub-infeudated to a mesne lord who was also lord of Wykham, Epwell and Swalcliffe, and through him to other knights. In the early thirteenth century one fee in Fawler was held by Thomas Caperon who also had a manor in Epwell; another in Fawler and Finstock was held by the heirs of Robert le Chevalchesul who also had land in Swalcliffe; and a third in Fawler was held by the le Blunds who owed allegiance to Wykham.[39] The northern manors and those in the woodland could have been granted independently, but it seems much more likely that the northern manor and the 'wood' belonged together, and that the agreement with the lord of Swalcliffe La Lea recognized a right in the woodland which persisted in law even though most of Fawler had by that time been acquired by Eynsham Abbey.

The evidence is incomplete, and unfortunately there is none at all regarding rights of common held by or in Witney manor, but there is sufficient information to show both the degree of intercommoning, and the separation of the two woodland pasture areas. The division between the two corresponds almost exactly to the line of Grim's Ditch, although Finstock and Ramsden are anomalous in being situated within the line of the Ditch but having rights in western Wychwood.

Animals in the forest

Evidence as to which animals were allowed into the Forest is usually late in date and often contradictory, but pigs were undoubtedly permitted in the time of mast since pannage payments are recorded in the Pipe Rolls, the Hundred Rolls, and an Eyre in 1637.[40] In the same Inquiry it was stated that goats were not allowed, but this may not have applied in the medieval period since in 1232 the men of Stonesfield, Combe and Hanborough petitioned to 'have their goats in the Forest as they used to in the time of King John'.[41] In western Wychwood sheep were allowed in the royal woods in the large specified and marked sheepwalks,[42] but there is no definite evidence regarding the Grim's Ditch area. In the post medieval period it seems almost certain that sheep used the pasture within the woodland, since in 1607 Stonesfield tenants holding only very small parcels of land were each allowed 25 sheep, while several were allowed 100 or more, to a total of 2,000 sheep for a small parish with only 260 acres of arable.[43] This may not have been the situation earlier, but woodland sheep runs are known to have existed in Charlbury, and some tenants in Taston (in Spelsbury) are recorded as having, in addition to their customary stint, sheep without number in le Serte, suggesting a tradition of unrestricted pasturing of sheep in the woodland there.[44] The existence of early fulling mills at Cleveley (in Enstone), Minster and Witney also supports the idea that for the local inhabitants the sheep may have been the most important of the animals grazing in Wychwood.[45]

Cattle and horses were also pastured there, apparently without any geographical restriction, but the 1792 Report states that cattle were limited in number. They were, by custom, turned in to the Forest in the spring and taken out again in late autumn and each commoner was supposed to graze no more that he could support throughout the winter.

The evidence discussed in this and the preceding chapter suggests that Wychwood in the Norman period was a closely defined area of woodland, every part of which was subject to various legal and customary rights, and this background must be borne in mind in any consideration of the changes which took place in the three centuries following the Conquest.

5

Wychwood after 1086

As has already been hinted in the previous chapters, the amount of assarting in Wychwood after 1086 was less than once thought, and it is also apparent that there was not a uniform expansion into the woodland, but that assarting was restricted to specific areas and to certain periods.

The process of assarting has been summarized in Table 3 above, and this shows that in the twelfth century assarts were made at the woodland edge in Stanton and also possibly in Langley and Charlbury, but that most of the assarting took place in the Grim's Ditch vills south of the Evenlode (Finstock c.1140, North Leigh 1190, Ramsden — or possibly Leafield — 1199), thus enlarging what was already the largest clearing in the woodland.[1]

During the following century assarting continued in that area and in south-east Wychwood, although in the latter area the assarts were never large and the process was probably complete before 1270 when Hanborough's 38 acres of old assart were recorded.[2] Further assarts were recorded for North Leigh and Finstock, and 120 acres of wood were cut down to provide additional arable for Ramsden.[3] The greater part of the clearance, however, took place in Hailey, where there were 475 acres of assart land in 1237 and another 175 acres by 1279.[4] Eventually there was no longer any wood separating the clearing in the Wilcote area from the fields beside the Windrush, and the woods of Cogges, Eynsham and Stanton had been cut off from the rest of Wychwood.

Another feature of the thirteenth century was the expansion of the arable on the northern bank of the Evenlode, in the royal vills of Combe, Stonesfield and Wootton. The tenants of Combe each held $18^1/_2$ acres of assart in 1279, and a further assart of 200 acres was made in 1298; while in Stonesfield the tenants each held 21 acres of new assart in 1279, and an assart in Wootton woods (of unspecified size) was also recorded at that date, with a further 80 acres assarted before 1300.[5] Some small assarts were also made in the adjacent non-royal woods in Fawler (recorded in 1272 and 1300), in Spelsbury (1279) and in Enstone (1276), but the great change in those woods followed the Perambulation of 1300, by which they were, in theory, disafforested.[6] The agreements regarding common rights, already mentioned, were made between the lords of inter-commoning manors, so that the right of common pasture was restricted to the time after the crop had been taken and to the fallow year. Large assarts were made in Charlbury (115 acres recorded in 1337, the total amount being about 330 acres), in Enstone (140 acres in 1307 and possibly another 40 or 60 around 1320), in Ditchley (200 acres in 1345)[7] and probably also in Spelsbury, although there is no record of these. There is a similar lack of records regarding Kiddington and Glympton, but it is likely that the assarts which gave rise to Glympton Assarts Farm and Kiddington Assarts Farm (now Wood Farm) were made at that time.[8] The vills of western Wychwood, however, did not avail themselves of the opportunity provided by the 1300 Perambulation, except in the vicinity of Langley and Leafield, and a possible explanation of this is discussed later.

The king's influence on assarts

The variation in the date and site of the assarts was no doubt due to a combination of factors, and one of these, the soil type, probably provided the limiting factor in south-east Wychwood, for example. But where the soil was more suitable for agriculture the presence or absence of assarts must have depended on human factors, and in a royal Forest the most important of these was the king. The king's influence was felt at two levels, firstly through decisions made on a national scale, such as alterations in the Forest Law or in the boundaries of the Forest, and secondly in his role as a local landlord.

The various manorial woods were always within the Forest boundary until 1300 and so under the supervision of the Forester unless the lord was granted the privilege of having his woods freed from regard. This may have depended to some extent on the wealth or influence of that lord, but it was probably principally determined by the changing pattern of royal interest in the region.

In 1086 the king owned, in addition to his demesne forests, the hundredal manors of Shipton, Wootton and Bloxham, and at the same date he probably also held the estates which were recorded as belonging to Odo, bishop of Bayeux, including the demesne manors of Combe and Stanton and the overlordship of Bladon. In the following centuries Bloxham manor was first farmed, and later granted away, while Shipton manor was granted away very early, even though it was the largest and wealthiest of the royal manors.[9] Meanwhile, however, the king built up his estate around the park and palace of Woodstock, acquiring by escheat or exchange the manors of Bladon, Combe, Hanborough, Stonesfield, and both manors in Wootton. The palace of Woodstock was frequently reconstructed, enlarged or beautified[10] and there is no doubt that it played an important part in the lives of the medieval kings, being not only a good hunting centre but also a convenient resting place in the numerous journeys throughout England made by those monarchs. Itineraries of the kings show that there was hardly a year when Woodstock was not visited on at least one occasion, and sometimes the visits were of two to three weeks' duration.[11] The king could not fail to be aware of what was happening in the region, and presumably he acquiesced in, or even encouraged, the assarts of the twelfth and thirteenth century in the central portion of the Forest. He was probably the instigator of the thirteenth-century assarts to the north of the Evenlode since most of these were made in the royal vills, under the orders of the bailiff of Woodstock Manor.[12] Some of these assarts may have been linked to the development of the borough of

Table 5. Assarts and the ownership of the manor.

Lord	Assarts	Small assarts	No assarts
King	Combe Stonesfield Wootton	Hanborough	Bladon Bloxham*
Forester	Langley Leafield		
Church	Charlbury Enstone Fawler* Finstock* Hailey (Witney) North Leigh*	Crawley (Witney) Eynsham	Taynton Widford
Lay	Bloxham* Fawler* Finstock* Fulbrook † Glympton Kiddington North Leigh* Ramsden Spelsbury Stanton	Cogges ? Chilson	Ascott Asthall Chadlington Fulbrook Minster Pudlicote Sarsden Swinbrook Wilcote

* Change of ownership during the period 1086-1400.
† Assarted to provide arable for Leafield.

Woodstock, since one large assart in Wootton's wood was held by Edmund de Wodestoke, and other men from Woodstock held land in the Combe assart of 1298.[13]

It seems likely that by this time most of the deer in this particular area had been confined within Woodstock Park. Men of the neighbourhood certainly complained about damage done by deer which escaped from the park in 1231, and in 1276 the abbot of Winchcombe claimed that Enstone's wood was '2 leagues distant from the covert and not a resort of deer'.[14] Since he was applying for permission to assart there, this statement may not have been correct, and in 1306 deer were said still to be found in the abbot of Eynsham's wood of Charlbury, near by. They were, however, not in such numbers as in his wood at Finstock, while in the woods of Eynsham itself they were said to be found only rarely.[15] By 1300, then, the deer were probably more or less restricted to Woodstock Park and to the woodland of western Wychwood. This too may have been the result of a royal policy of keeping that area as a game reserve and as a source of timber and other woodland products. The estate at Cornbury, for example, remained undeveloped; in the fourteenth century it was a stud for the king's horses, and occasionally it was called upon to provide timber for the king's works or royal gifts; but the greater part of that was obtained from the demesne woodland, as also were supplies of brushwood and charcoal for Woodstock Palace, and other products such as hurdles, 1,000 of which were ordered in 1266.[16]

The provision of this wood, timber and charcoal, and of venison for the king's larder, was the responsibility of the Forester, who appears to have exercised almost complete control over the demesne wood-land.[17] It is perhaps significant that most of the assarts in this part of the Forest were made in the two vills which were directly under the Forester's influence, Langley itself and Leafield. John de Langley was responsible for one assart in Leafield, that 'between Felda and Lovebyri' (the area later known as Clay Assarts and Watcham Sart), and he also assarted almost all the remaining woodland at Langley, so that in 1331 his successor, Thomas de Langley, paid relief on '95 acres of assart in divers places in the Forest of Whicchewude'.[18]

The propinquity of the Forester, and the presence of large numbers of deer, may have been the reasons why the vills in western Wychwood did not avail themselves of the opportunity to assart offered by the 1300 Perambulation; but there is a more cogent reason why they should not have cut down their woods, and this was the possible loss of their rights of common in the large area of royal demesne wood-land. Edward I laid down in 1305 that:

in regard to those whose lands and tenements are disafforested
by the said perambulation and who demand to have common

within the bounds of the forests, the king's intention and will is, since they claim to be quit by the perambulation of the puture of the foresters and that the king's beasts may not have their haunt or repair on the lands disafforested as they had when their lands were within the forest, that these men ought not to have common or easement within the bounds of the forest. But if any of those who are disafforested by the perambulation would rather be within the forest as they were before than outside as they are now, the king is well pleased that they shall be received, to the end that they may remain in their ancient estate and have common and other easements within the forest as they had before.[19]

The vills of western Wychwood presumably valued their rights of common in the demesne woodland highly, since they refrained from making any changes in the use of their own woodland.

Other influences on assarting

The general picture of assarting in the region thus seems to have been controlled to some extent by the king; but within the limits set by royal policy it might be thought that the expansion or otherwise of a manor would depend on the will of the person next in importance, the lord of that manor. Variations between manors would thus be expected, but in the Wychwood region the lords in any given area appear to have pursued very similar policies regardless of differences in their status, influence or wealth.

Writers on the subject of post-Conquest expansion have sometimes distinguished between manors held by lay lords and those held by the Church, and it is usually believed that monasteries and other ecclesiastical lords were responsible for the greater part of the changes which took place. In Wychwood this seems to be true but it is almost entirely due to the fact that the Church held many of the manors with the greatest potential for development. The woodland of Witney manor, for example (held by the bishop of Winchester), was 3 leagues long and 2 leagues wide, and second in size only to the king's demesne woodland.

In other cases the amount of assarting attributed to ecclesiastical institutions has been exaggerated, and Eynsham Abbey provides a good example of this. One writer has even implied that the Abbey (founded in 1005) brought into existence the villages of Church Hanborough, North Leigh and Combe,[20] all of which were well established by 1066, with archaeological evidence suggesting much earlier origins. It has also been said that the increase in size of the demesne at Eynsham itself, from 3 ploughs in 1086 to $8^1/_2$ hides in 1279 and 14 hides in 1360, was brought about by assarting,[21] but Sir Edmund Chambers pointed out that 'if we compare the Survey of 1279 with that of 1086 it becomes apparent that there had been no great change in the extent of arable cultivation',[22] and the increase in the demesne appears to have been at the expense of existing arable land which had earlier been held by tenants. In 1086 there was land for 18 ploughs of which 3 were in demesne, and the rest of the land was shared between three knights, who probably each held at least a hide, and 35 villeins, each of whom probably held a virgate since that was the usual tenement size in 1279.[23] At the latter date the total arable amounted to just over 17 (calculated) hides, very close to the 18 ploughlands of Domesday, but of that land only 23 virgates were held by villein tenants and $9^1/_2$ virgates (including one 1-hide tenement) by free tenants, the rest forming the demesne.[24] By 1360 the lord's holding had been swollen by the addition of land previously held by the many tenants who died in the Black Death, and since it also seems probable that the abbot acquired the greater part of the $1^1/_2$-hide Domesday manor of Pereio, it is unnecessary to ascribe the increase in size of his holding to assarting when there was little other evidence for this.[25]

In the Abbey's other manor of Charlbury there is no doubt that assarts were made, and that the abbots and their stewards were responsible for these, but estimates of the amount of assarting have usually assumed that Fawler and Finstock arose *de novo* in the post-Conquest period whereas it is almost certain that there were already settlements there in 1086. Eynsham Abbey did not in fact gain control of these vills until 1205 (Finstock) and 1230 (Fawler) when the estates were each described as $^1/_2$ knight's fee and were clearly already well developed.[26] Assarts in those vills in the latter part of the fourteenth century were in line with assarts in the adjoining manors, so that the Abbot was in no way a leader in the development of the area, but merely followed the general trend.

The ecclesiastic who does stand out as a pioneer is the bishop of Winchester who was paying money to the crown for assarts, presumably in Hailey, in 1209 and 1212, and it is possible, although not certain, that payments recorded in the earlier Pipe Rolls were also for assarts.[27] During the thirteenth century the pace of assarting was very rapid, and Patricia Hyde in her study of Witney Manor has linked the assarts in Hailey with the development of the bishop's new town at Witney, since a Custumal of 1237 and the Hundred Rolls show that most of the newly assarted land was held by the burgesses. The later assarts were not as closely linked to the borough.[28]

It is noticeable that even in manors where large areas were assarted a considerable amount of woodland remained, for example Abbot's Wood (later known as Lee's Rest Wood) in Charlbury and Fawler, the woods of Witney Chase in Crawley, and the royal woods in Stonesfield and Wootton. These woods were needed both as a source of wood and timber for the upkeep of the manor, and as wood-pasture for its animals, but the lords had an additional reason for preserving their woods, in the hope that they might be permitted to hold them as a chase or park where they would have the privilege of hunting. This was granted to the bishop of Winchester in 1284,[29] and in 1297 John Lovell applied for permission to impark the adjacent wood in Minster. This was presumably refused since a further, successful application was made by William Lovell in 1442.[30] Another small park was created in Stanton in 1329 when John Wyard was given licence to impark the wood belonging to the smaller manor there,[31] but these were probably the only private parks or chases in Wychwood in the medieval period.

Who used the assarts?

Very little of the newly assarted land was used to increase the size of the lord's demesne. This happened to a small extent in Charlbury and Stanton,[32] and at Langley and Ditchley which were atypical in consisting almost entirely of demesne, but elsewhere the assarts were held by the tenants, and it is hard to judge whether the lord's development of his manor was motivated solely by the desire for increased rents or was a response to pressure from those tenants. In the case of Witney the first is the more likely explanation, but in some other manors the second may have been of at least equal importance; and perhaps the best indication of the role of the tenants is to be found in the form taken by the assarts. These could be of three main types: the first was the separate farm carved out of the woodland, usually by a free tenant under licence from the lord; the second, the small enclosure located at the edge of the existing arable and held by one man, either free or villein; and the third, the large field divided into strips and shared by all or many of the villein tenants of a manor. All three types are found in the Wychwood region, but the third is the most usual, producing the irregular field systems described by H. L. Gray in his pioneer work on the subject.[33]

The evidence for this type of assart is particularly clear for Combe where all the customary tenants held $18^1/_2$ acres of assart in 1279, the 200 acres assarted in 1298 were shared between 35 tenants, and in 1609 the three assart fields of Wootton Sartes, Stevens Sarte and Coome Old Sarte were all described as common fields and shared by several men.[34] The assarts in Charlbury and Fawler appear in the Forest records as small holdings assigned to individual tenants, but in total they account for large areas, and in 1609 again they appear as assart fields shared by several men.[35] Many of the strips of the medieval assarts in Charlbury were still visible in the Tithe Award map, while the resemblance between the original fields and the assarts is shown by the fact that in the Victoria County History account of the manor a normal two- or three-field system is suggested.[36] In North Leigh also almost every customary tenant held a small piece of assart in 1279, but by 1581 those assarts were indistinguishable in form from the other fields of the manor,[37] and the later assarts in Ramsden and Leafield also took the form of large fields divided into strips. Hailey's assart land was in closes by 1609, but much of the inclosure had taken place in the Tudor period, and in the fourteenth century a tenant's holding of assart land could consist of small parcels in different places. In 1609 Delly Sarte was still shared by five men, suggesting that some at least of the assarts there may have been divided into strips as elsewhere.[38]

The second type of assart is most noticeable in Leafield, where in the early fourteenth century assarts of one or two acres are recorded for a few individuals,[39] but the first type, the separate farm within the woodland held by a free tenant, is rare in Wychwood. They possibly occurred in Kiddington, Wootton and Glympton, though common fields for the hamlet of Boriens are also recorded.[40] In these manors, however, there is a good geographical reason why an assart should have taken this form, in that the newly cleared land was separated from the old common fields by distance or a steep-sided valley, while elsewhere it was usually adjacent to the existing arable, so that co-operative assarting by a number or all of the villein tenants, directed by the lord or his steward, was the logical form of development.

It follows that the holder of the assart land in Wychwood was most commonly a tenant of villein status, in contrast to some other areas of England where the greater part of the assarting has been ascribed to the efforts of individual free tenants.[41] One feature of the assarts in Wychwood, however, is that the persons involved were not always inhabitants of the vill concerned. Of the seven men responsible, with the Steward of Shipton manor, for the Hulwerk assart in Ramsden, four came from the hamlet itself, but two from Hailey and one from Ascott,[42] and the Hundred Rolls and Forest records show other instances of men from one vill holding small pieces of assart in another, especially in Hailey, Ramsden, Finstock and Fawler, and it is clear that they acquired land wherever they could with scant regard for manorial boundaries.[43]

Manor	Demesne		Villein %	Free %	Assarts
	Size	%			
Walcot	2	31	–	69	–
Swinbrook	2	38	–	62	–
Chadlington Wahull	2	25	28	47	–
Sarsden	2	22	22	46	–
Pudlicote	2	28	28	44	–
Shipton	3	14	45	41	–
Chadlington Shippenhull	2	21	42	37	–
Hanborough	2	17	53	30	A
Cogges	2	42	29	29	?
Asterleigh	2	31	42	27	A
Glympton	2	30	43	27	A
Minster	3	33	41	26	–
Ascott	4	31	44	25	–
Asthall	2	22	55	23	–
Fulbrook	3	29	50	21	–
Enstone	5	19	60	21	AA
Finstock	–	–	80	20	A
Hailey	–	–	80	20	AAA
Spelsbury	3	20	62	18	A
Nether Kiddington	2	28	56	16	A
Eynsham	8½	50	35	15	A
Bladon	2	36	50	14	–
Taynton	2	20	66	14	–
Fawler	2	27	60	13	AA
North Leigh	3	27	64	9	AA
Charlbury	4	48	48	4	AA
Langley	3	92	8	–	AA
Stanton	8	49	51	–	A
Combe	1	25	75	–	AA
Crawley	1	25	75	–	A
South Leigh	–	–	100	–	A
Stonesfield	–	–	100	–	A
Leafield) Ramsden)	all land in acres, no demesne or villein tenements				

The table is arranged according to the percentage of the total number of virgates in the township held by the free tenants in 1279. Assart land not included. A, AA and AAA indicate roughly quantitative estimates of the amount of assarting in each vill.

A   assart at any date during the period under study. Size of demesne is given in carucates or hides.

Table 6. Assarts related to township social structure, 1279.

Population growth and the hunger for land

Land hunger of this type is commonly attributed to the pressure of 'a great expansion of the rural population',[44] the reason usually given for the assarts made in the post-Conquest period. Some idea of population changes in the region can be obtained from table 7, which includes post-medieval figures as indications of the potential of the manors. Lyneham and Kingham are included as examples of neighbouring manors with no woodland available for assarting, and manors for which there is no Domesday entry, or the Domesday figures cannot easily be related to those of later dates, have been placed at the bottom of the table.

It can be seen that although there was a general increase in the population in the region between 1086 and 1279, this increase was by no means uniformly distributed, since in a large number of manors there was very little change (in some cases there was an apparent decrease), and this stability — or stagnation — lasted in many cases until the nineteenth century. In others the population did increase but this finding may in part be due to the nature of the statistics. Both Domesday Book and the Hundred Rolls are primarily records of holders of land (although some landless cottagers are included), and they immediately create a population difference between manors in which assart land was available and those in which there was no assarting. The former could appear more populous merely because of the number of small pieces of assart land held by tenants of other manors or by young men of the manor who would otherwise be unrecorded sub-tenants or landless labourers.

Some of the increase may, however, have been real, and while this could have originated within the manor, it is also possible that the availability of assart land caused an influx of men from elsewhere. This contradicts the traditional view that the medieval peasant was bound to his manor, but it is impossible to account for the growth of Witney, for example, unless this happened. If locative surnames can be trusted as an indication of origin, the thirteenth-century assarts there

Manor	1086	1279	% change	1327	1642	1801
Asthall	40	32	−20	34	81	304
Asterleigh &						
Kiddington	27	42	+55	11	46	189
Bladon	28	24	−14	14	−	287
Eynsham	70	50	−29	55		1,166
Fulbrook	41	32	−22	38	52	320
Glympton*	26	28	+8	19	31	96
Milton*	8	(8)		35	92	495
Minster	33	42	+27	24	49	283
Spelsbury	42	55	+31	46	118	509
Stanton and						
South Leigh	95	99	+4	112	202	744
Taynton*	51	49	−4	26	69	315
Widford	11	−		4	−	45
Wilcote	2	6		−	6	9
Lyneham†	43	50	+16	44	44	195
Kingham†	43	48	+12	32	101	315
Ascott	27	64	+137	37	79	410
Combe	14	45	+222	26	96	424
Enstone	42	79	+90	81	124	912
Hanborough*	31	89	+155	71	−	655
North Leigh	42	116	+176	45	109	517
Stonesfield	6	29	+363	18	55	374
Swinbrook	7	21	+200	16	31	132
Witney (total)	56	376	+571	145	610	4,087
Total‡	766	1,376	+78			
Chadlington	−	60		58	109	593
Charlbury	−	25		45	193	965
Cogges	?3	41		35	79	343
Fawler	−	9		24	22	112
Finstock	−	14		14	58	326
Leafield	−	13		32	73	487
Ramsden	−	37		13	42	335
Sarsden	−	20		14		92
Shipton		55		25	104	406

1086 and 1279   total of recorded tenants
1327   taxpayers
1642   males over 18, Protestation Returns
1801   Census Returns, total population
The Poll Taxes of the late fourteenth century are so incomplete as to be unhelpful, and have been omitted. The manors are grouped according to whether there was less or more than the average increase in 'population'.

*   probable change in size of manor, 1086–1279
†   manors with no Domesday woodland
‡   total excludes Widford and Milton

Table 7. 'Population' in the Wychwood region.

were taken up by men who came from Standlake, Lew, Stanton, Woodstock, Abingdon, Minister, Hanborough, Binsey, Asthall, Yarnton and Ducklington.[45] All of these are within reasonable distance of Witney, but none belonged to the bishop, so that there was no possibility that the men were merely transferred by him from one of his manors to another.

Witney is, however, rather a special case since the assarting was presumably directed by the bishop for his own purposes and was not directly related to population pressure within either the manor or the region. Since it seems possible that in the other vills the population figure given in 1279 was the result of assarting rather than its cause, some other means must be found of estimating whether an excess of population existed within individual manors. Such an indication may be provided by the most common form of villein tenement, assuming that the virgate was the norm and that half-virgate holdings arose as the result of fission. This assumption seems reasonable, since the Hundred Rolls for the region show several examples of tenements described as virgates but shared by two tenants, apart from those in which the holding is called a half-virgate.[46] Information regarding the numbers and types of the villein tenements in 1279 is given in table 8, and it can be seen that in seven vills all the land was held in virgates, these being mainly the 'stable' vills of western Wychwood. In Stonesfield and Minster, however, all the customary land was in the form of half-virgates, as was almost all of that in Cogges and North Leigh. The distinction between the two types of holding would be unimportant if the virgate were much larger in one manor than in another, but wherever evidence is available it suggests that the virgate was larger in the manors where the virgate tenement was the rule, and that it was small where the half virgate was the usual form of holding, so that the imbalance was even greater than expected.[47] In some manors there were in 1279 tenants whose holdings were even smaller than half a virgate (for example, 31 in North Leigh and 22 in Stonesfield) suggesting poor and overcrowded villages.[48] The demand for land in those manors was not satisfied by assarting within the

Manor	½ Virgate*	Virgate	Cottars etc.	Assarts
Chadlington Shippenhull	–	16	–	–
Chadlington Wahull	–	9	–	–
Enstone	–	63	–	AA
Finstock	–	4	8	A
Nether Kiddington	–	15	1	A
Sarsden	–	8	6	–
Shipton	–	35	8	–
Asthall	3	11	5	–
Asthall Leigh	2	10	–	–
Spelsbury	10	33	6	A
Eynsham	6	20	4	–
Fulbrook	7	21	4	(A)
Taynton	15	25	–	–
Hailey	10	17	–	AAA
Bladon	6	8	3	–
South Leigh	14	15	–	A
Pudlicote	4	4	–	–
Ascott	16	14	22	–
Glympton	7	5	6	A
Crawley	12	6	3	A
Stanton	21	7	1	–
Hanborough	31	10	5	A
Combe	12	3	24	AA
Cogges	10	1	5	–
North Leigh	54	2	31	AA
Stonesfield	11	–	22	A
Minster	30	–	–	–
Leafield	} land held only in acres			AA
Ramsden	}			AA

The table is arranged according to the relative proportion of virgate/½-virgate holdings.

No information is available for Charlbury and Fawler.

* tenements described as such, or virgate tenements shared by two men

A assarts at any time during the period under study; A, AA and AAA indicate roughly quantitative estimates of the amount of assarting in each vill.

Table 8. Assarts related to size of villein holdings, 1279.

manor since North Leigh men took up land in Hailey, Ramsden and Finstock, while Stonesfield men held an assart in Wootton woods in 1279, and even in 1609 were sharing one of Combe's assart fields with the men of that vill.[49]

These findings suggest that there was a direct relationship between the half virgate tenement and assarting within the manor, but this does not hold good everywhere, since there was no assarting in Minster, where the half-virgate was the only form of villein tenement. The fact that Minster's population changed very little between 1086 and 1279 suggests that the land was already held as half virgates at the earlier date, and it is possible that the half-virgate was the normal holding in the south-eastern part of Wychwood, where it predominates in almost every manor. In that case it may represent population pressure at an even earlier date, or possibly an economy not relying heavily on arable.[50]

The whole question of the relationship between the assarts and manorial organization and population is complex, but the statistics do point out a fundamental difference in the Wychwood region between the settlements in the river valleys, which had a stable population, an agricultural system based on two fields of equal size with the tenants' holdings in virgates, and little or no assarting, and the 'forest' vills, where a number of villeins held half a virgate or less, where assarting led to the development of irregular field systems, and where manorial boundaries seem to have been of little importance.

Other work within (and without) the law

In view of their small holding of arable, it seems certain that many of the inhabitants of the 'forest' villages must have had by-employments, although there is very little medieval evidence for these. Fifteen men were recorded under Langley in 1279 as holding only a messuage, and some of these presumably assisted the Forester in his duties.[51] One of these was the making of charcoal, and the surname Collier found in the region then and later testifies to that occupation. There was also some illegal charcoal-burning — men from Ditchley, Finstock and

Ramsden were imprisoned for that offence in 1272.[52]

Another form of illegal use of the woodland is recorded in 1245 when the Attachments for Vert detail numerous examples of the cutting of trees (mainly oaks, although hazel and thorn are also mentioned), men from Walcot, North Leigh and Slape being the chief offenders. In Walcot and Slape in particular the same names recur both as offenders and pledges, and it seems likely that in these vills there were groups of men who supplemented their living by woodcutting, and that the fine was possibly in the nature of a licence fee. Further offences against the vert are recorded in 1256 and 1272, at which date the tenants of almost every village in and around the woodland were accused of taking carts into the woods belonging to the king and other lords and carrying away wood and underwood 'to Oxford and other markets'.[53] In this connection it is interesting to note that the same complaint about the plundering of the woodland by the inhabitants of the Forest villages was made in 1792, and many were fined for it in 1848.[54] Some poaching of deer was also recorded in the thirteenth-century records, although the offender was as likely to be the lord of a manor or his woodward as to be any of the humbler inhabitants.[55]

The folios of the Forest records suggest that the Forest villages were rather lawless communities, and the same opinion was held in the nineteenth century when one writer described 'a dangerous species of semi-barbarous freedom produced by large tracts of woodland' and 'a race of the poor who cannot bear the thought of work while surrounded by such prolific wastes'.[56] Whether this is true or not, it nevertheless seems likely that the inhabitants of those settlements relied on the woodland to a far greater extent than those of the river-valley villages, and to them the assarting of that woodland must have seemed a disturbing and revolutionary process.

The end of assarting

The result of almost three centuries of assarting is as shown in map 14, with the more or less continuous woodland of 1086 divided into three areas, the woods of western Wychwood, the wood and heath,

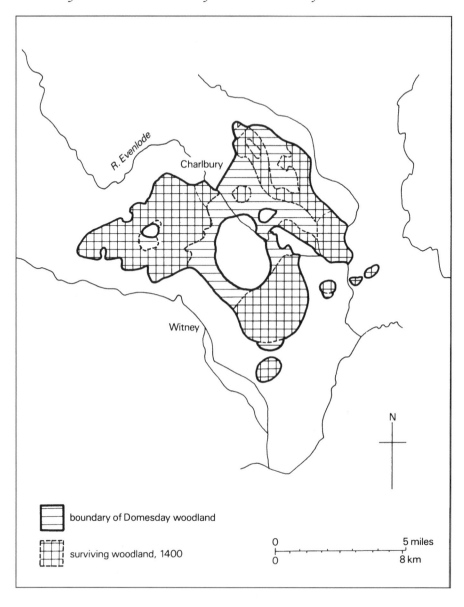

Map 14. Changes in the woodland, 1086–c.1400.

with some outlying woods, in south-east Wychwood, and an area of fragmented woods interspersed with arable and pasture north of the Evenlode, these being separated from each other by a continuous area of cleared land stretching from Witney to Charlbury.

Records of assarts cease around 1340, and although this may be due to the reduction in size of the Forest and increasingly careless administration, it seems likely that the impact of the Black Death on the region did bring assarting to an end. Tilgarsley, in Eynsham, was depopulated and never resettled, and in Stanton the lords of both manors died, and their Inquisitions Post Mortem record that many of their tenants had also died 'and their lands be untilled in the lord's hands because no-one is willing to buy or hire them'.[57] In Witney two-thirds of the population died, and the bishop of Winchester received 57 heriots from 63 tenements. In 1350 he still had in hand $15^{1}/_{2}$ virgates of customary land in Hailey, 3 virgates in Crawley, and 702 acres of assart land, and another outbreak of plague in 1361 added to the number of tenements in hand.[58]

An Inquisition in 1363 recorded that part of Finstock's arable was 'not measured or estimated because it is not cultivated these days', and Charlbury saw a decline in rents and profits of court in 1350, while in the time of Elizabeth I there were still 100 acres of 'decayed lands' there, probably the hamlet of Cote, which was never resettled.[59] The vills in the Glyme valley may not have been affected to the same extent, but there is evidence of a decline due to severe epidemics in the following century, and poverty and decrease in population were the reasons given for the amalgamation, in 1466, of the parishes of Asterleigh and Nether Kiddington.[60]

In these circumstances there was no need for further assarting, and apart from some minor encroachments on the heaths, there was little alteration in the amount of cleared land in the region until the Inclosures of the late eighteenth and nineteenth centuries.

6

The Forest after 1400

Although there was little alteration in the extent of the woodland of Wychwood in the four centuries after 1400, there were changes both in the ownership of estates in the area and in the extent and organisation of the Forest.

The principal changes in ownership came with the Dissolution of the Monasteries when the manors which had belonged to Eynsham Abbey and Winchcombe Abbey passed first to the Crown and then into the hands of individual landlords. Winchcombe's manor of Enstone was acquired by Sir Thomas Pope and passed to his heir, but by 1609 that part of the manor which had been woodland in 1086 was occupied by Sir Henry Lee. He had also acquired Ditchley (including Bloxham Wood) and the wooded part of Spelsbury, and so brought into being the Ditchley estate which still exists.[1]

Another change was the rise in importance of Cornbury. It must have been of some importance in the twelfth century since the annual rent for the Forest was paid under its name, not under Wychwood. Then and later it belonged to the Crown, and royal charters were signed there in 1105 and 1110,[2] but little else is recorded for it and in the period under study it seems to have been used by the kings mainly as a stud and a source of timber. The two centres of power in Wychwood then were Woodstock Park, the residence of the king or his bailiff, and Langley, home of the Forester. The last of the de Langleys, the hereditary Foresters, died in the fourteenth century and his estates, including Langley, eventually came into the hands of the

Crown. But although Henry VII built a hunting lodge there, it declined in local importance since the de Langleys' successors, the men to whom the keeping of the Forest was granted, were usually also granted the keeping of the park at Cornbury, and lived there. The two offices were often given to men of high status who were loyal servants of the Crown, and these included Robert, Earl of Leicester, favourite of Queen Elizabeth I, and Sir John Fortescue, her Chancellor. The house at Cornbury had been described in 1337 as a lodge, built of stone and timber, but it was probably rebuilt in the late fifteenth or early sixteenth century. In the seventeenth century it was altered or enlarged twice, always on a grander scale to suit the status of the holders. In 1661 Charles II rewarded his faithful Chancellor Edward Hyde, Earl of Clarendon, by giving Cornbury to him, and it has remained in private hands ever since.[3]

Woodstock palace continued to be used occasionally by the Tudor and Stuart kings, but the palace was damaged and the park despoiled in the Civil War and in 1706 it and the royal manors surrounding it were granted to the Duke of Marlborough.[4] This meant that the only remnant of the once extensive royal estates in the region was the demesne woodland, which was also the 'Forest of Wychwood' as it had been defined in 1622.

The changes in the extent of the legal Forest occurred in stages. The first change was during the period studied in the previous chapters, since in 1300 Edward I, under pressure from his nobles, agreed to disafforest land which the local landlords claimed had been falsely included within the Forest after the Charter of the Forest in 1217 and the perambulations which followed it. The knights who made the new perambulations which were to define the areas remaining within Wychwood divided it into three sections, the first consisting of the King's own manors and woodland around Woodstock Park, the second of Cornbury and the royal demesne woodland which adjoined it (although including the western part of Finstock), and the third the bishop of Winchester's two vills of Hailey and Crawley, with the western part of North Leigh. The perambulators stated that all the private woods outside those areas had been afforested since the date stipulated. The same happened in Forests all over England and the king naturally protested, even appealing to the Pope so that he could revoke these disafforestations. The Forests were, of course, a source of revenue in the fines imposed for infringements of the Forest law, and these would be much reduced. The perambulations were eventually accepted, but not until 1327, and even then some degree of royal control was exercised by the Forester over the disafforested areas which, in Western Wychwood at least, became known as the Purlieus.[5]

A re-arrangement of the oversight of the Forest was made *circa* 1480, with the declaration of a New Forest 'near and without the Park of Woodstock'. This was said to extend 'from the town of Charlbury to the said park, and from the water of Combe [the Evenlode] to the water of Glyme', and as a result control of that area was taken away from the Forester of Wychwood. It was given to the man who actually kept the royal woods around Woodstock, who usually was also the keeper of the King's palace and park there.[6] The New Forest is said to have been disafforested by Richard III, although a 'keeper of the New Forest' was recorded in 1609.[7]

The existence of the New Forest and its possible disafforestation were, however, ignored by a description of the bounds of Wychwood as recorded in a Survey of Langley Manor in 1552.[8] There the bounds of the Forest were said to be

> first from the wall of Wodestoke Park and thence to the Bridge called Bladenbridge and so by the water of Bladenbroke [Evenlode] to the water Mill of Eynsham [at the Eynsham-Hanborough boundary] and so to Grymsham [the island in the Windrush between Witney and Cogges] and so thence by the rivulet called Wynerusshewater to the bridge of the borough of Burford ... which extends in length 12 miles, and from the bridge of Burford by known limits and bounds to the water of Glyme and so thence to the wall of Woodstock Park, which extends in length 12 miles, in width in divers places 7 miles and in other places 1 mile.

This includes both the Forest as defined by the 1300 perambulations and the woods which had in theory been disafforested at that time, and shows that the Forester, at least, believed that he still controlled the whole area. However in 1596 the manors around Woodstock Park were described as 'within the old precincte of the Forest of Whichwood but not used or regarded as parcell of the same within the memory of man', and the local inhabitants believed that they were no longer within the Forest.[9]

When James I came to the English throne he wanted to raise his income from the Forests by increasing the sums paid for the lease of the coppices (see later), by re-imposing upon the Forest tenants assart rents which had lapsed, or by querying their title to the land they occupied.[10] The 1609 survey which is so valuable a source of information about the Forest at this date was made in connection with this action by the king. Apart from detailing the area which the king claimed as Forest, it names the landowners and occupiers at that date, and the most influential of these were Sir Henry Lee, who was Steward of Woodstock and keeper of the New Forest as well as holding Ditchley, and Sir Francis Fortescue, the Ranger (Forester) of Wychwood, who held Cornbury and Langley and also leased from the Crown the coppices in the demesne woodland.[11]

It is not known when the practice of leasing out the royal coppices began, but it remained a feature of the management of Wychwood until the Disafforestation. There were twenty coppices and the lessee would cut the underwood in one of them each year and sell it, keeping back a certain amount with which a fence was built to protect the coppice from the depredations of the deer and the commoners' animals for seven years while the wood was growing again. From the profits of the sale a fixed sum was paid to the Crown and the lessee kept any excess. This system led to some abuse both by the lessees and by the local tenants, and a survey of the coppices made in 1617 stated that they had 'bene formerlie muche abused and neglected', some of them had been felled at the wrong time and most of them were 'muche spoyled by browsing' since the fences were deliberately removed or opened up too early.[12] James I was optimistic to think that he would be able to extract more revenue from a Forest in such poor condition.

His other attempt to raise revenue, from assart rents or from payments for certainty of title, caused considerable discontent, especially in the Woodstock area.[13] Many tenants did pay a composition to the Crown, but a further perambulation in 1622 restricted the Forest to the area of royal demesne woodland stretching in a south-westerly direction from Cornbury Park towards Swinbrook and Widford.[14] In spite of this, Charles I continued to claim that the Forest extended to

the towns of Old and New Woodstock, Bladon, Easham, Stanton Harcourt, Southleigh, Cogges, Witney, Widford, Langley, Minster Lovell, Shipton under Whichwood, Pudlicote, Fyfield, Taynton, Idbury, Bruerne, Sarsden, Deane, Chadlington, Spellsbury, Charlbury, Fawler, Willcote, Northleighe, Hamborowe, Combe, Stonesfield, Dytchleye, Taston, Fulwell, Neat Enstone, Clyveley, Radford, Upper Kiddington, Asterley, Glympton, Wootton and Hordley and their precincts"

— a reversion to the extent of the Forest as it had been in the thirteenth century, and an even greater area than his father had claimed. However in 1641 he was forced to agree with the bounds as described in 1622, and this is the area which remained as the Forest of Wychwood for the next two centuries.[15]

Towards the end of the eighteenth century reports were submitted to Parliament on all of the Forests which remained in the hands of the Crown.[16] The Tenth Report, presented in 1792, dealt with Wychwood, and found that it was in an unsatisfactory condition from the Crown's point of view, mainly because the management of the Forest was divided between three persons or bodies. The first was the Ranger, the successor to the mediaeval Forester. He was principally responsible for the deer and for the open Forest, the area between the coppices, although he was also involved in the fencing of the coppices when they were felled. At that date the position was held by the Duke of

Marlborough. The Crown got very little profit from the deer since, of the 100 or more killed annually, only six went to the King. As in the seventeenth century, the profits from the woodland were less than they should have been, partly due to the fact that its management had been divided between two government departments, the Surveyor of Woods being principally interested in the timber (for the navy, above all, at that time) and the Department of Crown Lands in the leasing of the coppices or sale of the underwood. No one person or body was responsible for seeing that the Forest was properly cared for. In the Report it was proposed that an official should be appointed to live in the Forest for that purpose, and also that the Duke of Marlborough's rights should be bought out and the leases of the coppices not renewed so that the growth of timber would be encouraged.

However, little appears to have been done, and in 1807 Arthur Young, in his *General View of the Agriculture of Oxfordshire*, wrote: 'I did not see one very fine tree of navy oak in a ride of 16 or 17 miles' through the Forest. He advocated that it should be cleared altogether and converted to agriculture.[17]

In 1819 it was proposed that this should be done, but there was strong opposition from the Ranger and others with property and interests in and near the Forest. The management of the Forest was later hindered by a disagreement as to his rights between the Crown and Lord Churchill, a younger son of the Duke of Marlborough, who was the Ranger of Wychwood at that date. This dispute prevented all timber cutting for about twenty years, and led to a long and expensive legal suit which was brought to an end only by the death of Lord Churchill in 1845 and his son's agreement to compromise. Another government report on the Forest in 1848 was in favour of Disafforestation followed by enclosure for agriculture, as Arthur Young had suggested, rather than for the growth of timber as advocated fifty years earlier. The evidence in the report emphasised that Leafield, situated in the middle of the woodland, was 'very good corn land', although at that time the crops were much damaged by deer, and that 'every 100 acres of Forest, if enclosed, would give employment to about four labourers, permanently, rather than the casual and uncertain employment at the time'. In true Victorian fashion the writers of the report supported their argument for Disafforestation and clearance by claiming that there was 'a considerable demoralisation of the population of the district which nothing but the intervention of Parliament will radically cure',[18] and Arthur Young had also criticised the people living around the Forest, writing that

> the vicinity is filled with poachers, deer-stealers, thieves and pilferers of every kind — Oxford gaol would be uninhabited were it not for this fertile source of crime.

Whatever the arguments for Disafforestation, by this date it had probably been agreed that Wychwood was an anachronism and should be done away with. Other royal Forests (Hainault, Whittlewood and Woolmer) were disafforested around the same date.[19]

After a certain amount of consultation with local landowners[20] a *Bill for Disafforesting the Forest of Whichwood* was introduced to Parliament in 1853, followed by the *Whichwood Forest Amending Act* in 1857. By these two acts not only were the 3700 or more acres of royal Forest disafforested and divided into allotments, but the purlieu woods were also involved since some of their land was needed for the new roads and common allotments that were to be made. Those woods were freed from the Crown's forestal rights (of feed for the deer), and also from the rights in them which had been held by the inter-commoning villages.[21] The landowners of the purlieu villages then had only their own tenants to deal with, so that the Disafforestation opened the way for the clearance of their woods as well as the woodland of the royal Forest. Some did not choose to do this, but several did.

This, of course, meant a revolution in the life-style of many of the inhabitants of the area. Apart from any illegal activities, for the people of the surrounding villages the woodland of the Forest and its purlieus had provided feed for their animals, and dead wood, nuts and berries which were a welcome addition to their living, and these

Fairspear House, one of the new farmhouses built after disafforestation.

would no longer be available. It had also provided a certain amount of recreation, in the form of the annual Whitsun Hunt in which people from neighbouring villages participated, and which began a week of festivities, and the Forest Fair in autumn, which had begun as an innocent picnic for Witney Methodists but grew to be a rather riotous event.[22]

In all of the villages there must have been a sense of loss, but in Leafield, which was then completely surrounded by woods or the open forest, more than one-third of the adult male inhabitants in 1851 earned their living from those woods as woodmen, wood labourers, sawyers, hurdle-makers or game-keepers, and to them the clearance of the woodland would mean the loss of their livelihood and the end of a way of life which they and their ancestors had followed for centuries. This was not taken into consideration by the disafforesting Acts — presumably it was thought that they would adapt to the new conditions and work on the new farms. As it happened, many of them did, and Leafield itself acquired a handsome new church, its own policeman, and a draper and stationer's shop, amenities which it had not enjoyed previously.[23]

The loss of grazing within the forest which would be suffered by the tenants of the villages in the vicinity was compensated for by the allocation of some sheepwalks and special commons, one for each village, from the area to be inclosed. In the event these proved unworkable and they in their turn were inclosed and divided between the inhabitants of the villages by a series of Inclosure Awards between 1859 and 1863.[24] Part of one of these commons (originally made for the people of Minster Lovell) became the site of the new hamlet of Fordwells.[25]

The rest of the Forest was divided into two allotments, one of 1500 acres for Lord Churchill in compensation for his rights as Ranger, and the remainder for the Crown.

The Crown's allotment was rapidly cleared and converted into farms. This provided a last burst of activity for Leafield's woodmen, and the formidable task was accomplished very quickly, with less than two years between the passing of the Amending Act and the appear-ance of the first crops.[26] The farmhouses which were built on the Crown's allotment at that time still stand, some displaying the mono-grams of Queen Victoria and Prince Albert and the date (VR AP 1858) to prove their origin.[27] Other new farms came into being when most of the purlieu woods were also cut down, for example Riding Farm in Minster Lovell, Chasewood Farm in Crawley, and Dodd's Farm in Asthall.

Fordwells, a post-disafforestation village.

One writer of the day expressed his feelings in the words:

Poets and painters may sigh because some fine woodland scenery has been swept away; but of what consequence is a magnificent view when compared with that plenty which has now taken the place of poverty, or those habits of industry now firmly established where dissipation and crime once abounded.[28]

Today's readers may or may not agree.

Lord Churchill's allotment lay next to his home at Cornbury Park, and he and later owners have preferred to keep it in its wooded state. It provides the largest surviving remnant of the medieval woodland, although other scattered woods between the Windrush and the Glyme also remain to perpetuate the memory of Oxfordshire's great forest of Wychwood.

7

Re-writing the History

From the evidence discussed in the previous chapters one can build up a picture of Wychwood in the medieval period, and the main impression is less one of rapid and continuous change than of remarkable stability, especially in the western and south-eastern parts where there was hardly any alteration in the woodland between 1086 and the eighteenth or nineteenth century. To the north of the Evenlode, too, the general shape of the Domesday woodland is still discernible in maps, and much is still present in the landscape. Even in the triangle between Charlbury, Combe and Witney, where extensive assarts were made, these were usually enlargements of existing clearings with little sign of the creation of completely new settlements and field systems.

The place-name evidence suggests that the distribution of arable and woodland was much the same in the Saxon period, and this is supported by the small amount of archaeological evidence so far available. In view of the fairly intensive prehistoric and Roman occupation in the region, the question thus arises as to how and when the woodland, the woodland rights, the *leah* settlements, and the name Wychwood itself came into being.

It has been suggested that Wychwood was so called because it was the common wood-pasture of the early Saxon kingdom of the Hwicce.[1] That kingdom, eventually absorbed into Mercia, is recorded from AD 603, and its territory included much of Gloucestershire, Warwickshire and Worcestershire. Its boundary is thought to be represented by that of the medieval diocese of Worcester, since that diocese was created *circa* AD 675 to serve the kingdom; and the distribution of places named in charters associated with the kingdom or bishopric of the Hwicce confirms that belief.[2]

However, the diocesan boundary coincides with those of the counties of Gloucestershire and Warwickshire where they abut onto Oxfordshire, and it is clear that Wychwood did not belong to the Hwiccan kingdom in the late seventh century. If it ever had been part of that territory, it must have been separated from it before that date, and separated so completely that not one vestige of the presumed common or woodland rights remained to be recorded in the medieval period. On the contrary, W. J. Ford's work has shown that woodland rights and other tenurial links were contained entirely within the known territorial boundary of the Hwicce, and were sharply divided from the pattern of rights in Wychwood.[3] Oxfordshire west of the Cherwell could, of course, have earlier formed a self-contained unit within a larger tribal territory, but there is always the possibility that the name reflects not the situation in the Saxon period, but that at an earlier date. The Hwicce are thought to have included a considerable Romano-British element,[4] and in the Roman period there were at least economic links between the Wychwood region and Cirencester,[5] while even earlier both regions were in the territory of the Dobunni. This would, however, imply the existence of the woodland, the woodland rights, and possibly also the *leah* settlements in the Roman period or earlier.

With regard to the woodland, it is almost certain that some woods remained in the Roman period; the butt-ends of Grim's Ditch are thought to have run into woodland, and the bounds of the Ditchley villa estate are thought to have been formed by woods; while the economy of the Shakenoak villa always had a considerable pastoral element (cattle, sheep, pigs and goats), requiring a large amount of rough grazing, and the deer bones found at the site indicate the presence of woodland near by.[6] Possibly the 'regeneration of the woodland' in the post-Roman period was merely a matter of degree, in that some of the villa sites became overgrown, and arable fields reverted to rough scrub.[7]

As to the possibility that the *leah* sites already existed, considerable archaeological investigation is needed before any decision can be reached; but in connection with the woodland rights it is interesting to note the close links between the most heavily Romanized part of Wychwood, the Grim's Ditch area, and settlements in north Oxfordshire such as Swalcliffe and Bloxham which also have copious evidence of Roman occupation.[8] These, however, survived into the Saxon period as large and important estates,[9] so that one cannot be sure whether the woodland rights were retained from the Roman period or arose later. Of the other vills with detached woodland, Taynton was a royal possession before 1059 and has some evidence of Roman occupation, and Kidlington also has evidence of Roman occupation but its status in the Saxon period is not known; while Shipton was a Saxon royal vill and the head of a Hundred, but has (so far) only a small amount of evidence from the Roman period. There are, moreover, known Roman settlements in the vicinity, such as Chipping Norton,[10] which had no rights or interest in the woodland, so that the evidence is inconclusive.

However, independent evidence for the existence of well-defined woodland and woodland rights dating from the earliest phase of the Saxon settlement has been provided by two recent studies. The first is of the place-name Waltham (*Wealdham*) which seems to have been applied before AD 550 to royal estates which were concerned with the administration of woodland and possibly with hunting.[11] It occurs in several counties (although not in Oxfordshire) and in many cases the settlements have remains from the Roman period or earlier; and it seems more likely that such an institution already existed than that it appeared simultaneously in different parts of the country in the disturbed conditions of the fifth and sixth centuries. Similarly, the existence of detached woodland associated with large estates of Roman or earlier origin has been suggested by studies of the development of the Wolds.[12] Wychwood adds a small amount of information to the increasing volume of evidence for this aspect of landscape history, but it is not sufficient to formulate any convincing account, and further research into similar areas is needed before this will be achieved.

Other aspects of the medieval woodland may eventually throw some light on early history, and one of these is the tenurial structure. In Wychwood, as in Oxfordshire's other Forests of Shotover and Stowood, the woodland consisted of a central core owned directly by the king, surrounded by several compact manorial woods, all subject to common rights held by many vills. This type of organization differs markedly from that of the Weald of Kent and Sussex, where a manor's woodland consisted of several small 'dens' located along a drove road and intermingled with those of other manors,[13] while a third variant occurred in the Chilterns where there were manorial woods and areas of common pasture, but also numerous small woods held in severalty and belonging to the estates of individual owners, some only of villein status.[14]

These variations in tenurial organization are paralleled by differences in the physical structure of the woodland. Wychwood appears as consisting of numerous coppices, devoted to the growing of wood and underwood, [15] and the open forest which was used as pasture, and this type of arrangement was also found in Savernake and Rockingham.[16] However, there is no evidence in Wychwood for the separate *vaccaria* or dairy farms found in the New Forest and Inglewood, for example,[17] nor of the system of brecks (intermittent cultivation of some areas of the woodland) found in Sherwood.[18] Some of these differences must be due to variations in soil, terrain, or climate, but they could also reflect different cultural traditions.

Just as men affected the woodland, the presence of woodland influenced the lives of its inhabitants, and the contrast between the vills around Wychwood and those within it mirrors on a small scale that between the Felden and Arden areas of Warwickshire — on the one hand settled agricultural estates which changed little over the centuries, and on the other vills where both the amount of arable land

and the population increased in the medieval period. Even so, differences can be found, in that in Wychwood the assart land was used by tenants of villein status, and in Arden mostly by free men.

It seems certain that the study of any region will pose its own problems as to the distribution of the medieval woodland, the rights over it, the use made of it, and the way it developed; but 'an examination of the English woodland areas, and of the varied occupations and kinds of society to which they gave rise, is surely crucial to any understanding of the past'.[19]

Abbreviations

BAR   British Archaeological Reports

BL   British Library

Bodl   Bodleian Library, Oxford .

CBA   Council for British Archaeology

DB Oxfordshire   Domesday Book, Oxfordshire, ed. John Morris
               (History from the Sources,1978)

Eynsham Cartulary   Cartulary of Eynsham Abbey, ed. H. E. Salter (2
               vols., Oxford Historical Society: XLIX,1906-7, and LI,
               1908)

Oxf. Archives   Oxfordshire Archives, County Hall Oxford

PRO   Public Record Office

Rot. Hund.   Rotuli Hundredorum (Record Commission,1818)

Sites & Monuments Record   County Archaeology Sites and
               Monuments Record,Centre for Oxfordshire Studies,
               Central Library, Oxford

VCH   Victoria County History

Glossary

assart (verb) To clear a piece of land or wood for the purpose of agriculture. In a Forest this could be done only with the king's permission, and a payment had to be made to him for each crop sown.

bordar A manorial tenant of low status. There is a dispute as to whether he served in the lord's household (the name derived from an early form of "board") or on the fringes of the manor ("border"). In Shipton the latter seems much more likely.

brecks Land enclosed from the waste of a forest, usually on a temporary basis.

Custumal A written statement of the customs of a manor, the services owed by the free and unfree tenants, and the rights and obligations of their lord.

escheat The reversion of an estate to the lord or to the crown when the tenant died without heirs, or forfeited his estate because of a felony.

heriot A payment made to the lord of a manor on the death of a tenant. Usually the dead tenant's best beast, although sometimes a money payment.

hide The word has different meanings in different contexts. It is used principally as a measure of an area of arable land, in Oxfordshire usually about 120 acres although the size varies, with the rights to meadow, pasture, etc. belonging to it. Manors are described in terms of their hideage so that a 30-hide manor has approximately 30 times as much arable as a 1-hide estate. It was also a unit of taxation, although "beneficial hidation" could occasionally be found, when a manor was assessed at a lower number of hides for taxation purposes than the number of areal hides it contained.

hundred A division of a shire for administrative purposes, with an important manor (usually belonging to the king in the eleventh & twelfth centuries) as its centre.

intercommoning The system whereby the pasture in an area was used by the animals of several villages.

mereway A track forming the boundary (mere) between two woods or pieces of land.

mesne A term used for a lord who held estates from an overlord but granted some of them to minor lords. The minor lord then owed allegiance both to his mesne lord and to the overlord.

messuage A house with its associated outbuildings and yard.

oppidum A major Iron Age settlement surrounded by a series of banks and ditches.

pannage A payment made for the right to pasture pigs in the woods.

perambulation In the context of a Forest, a description of its bounds making a complete circuit and naming all the features of the boundary so that there would be no doubt what was inside and outside of the Forest. Usually perambulations were only made when some woods were to be disafforested and freed from royal control.

purlieu Land or wood once in a Forest but later disafforested

regard A triennial inspection of a Forest for the purpose of detecting any offences involving damage to the woodland there.

sheepwalk An area especially designated as pasture for sheep. Those in Wychwood near Langley and Leafield had boundary marks beyond which the shepherds were not permitted to let their sheep stray.

sub-infeudation The granting of a part of his estates by one lord to another, not absolutely but retaining his right as overlord.

vill General term used for a settlement, village or hamlet.

villein An unfree tenant holding land within a manor, for which he paid originally with labour services to the lord.

virgate A quantity of arable land with associated rights to meadow and pasture. It was one quarter of a hide, but the actual acreage could vary from place to place.

Ordnance Survey Maps

Maps 1 – 4 are taken from the Ordnance Survey map first published in 1833, with the railway added later.

Map 1

The map shows part of Cornbury Park and the Forest of Wychwood and its purlieus as they were in 1833, with the railway line added. The railway was not built until 1853, but it proved to be of great use for the transport of wood and timber when the woodland of Wychwood was eventually cleared.

The map shows how isolated Leafield was.

The distribution of wood and cleared land as shown in the upper part of this map had probably changed little since 1086. Changes did take place in the places shown in the lower part of the map, with assarts at Field Assarts, and in Ramsden, Hailey and Finstock. The remainder of the woodland shown here is much as it would have been in the Middle Ages, although the straight 'lights' or rides are post-medieval, cut to enhance the vistas. By way of contrast, the straight tracks in the lower half of the map are certainly (Akeman Street) or almost certainly (Pay Lane) Roman in origin.

Some of the coppices in the Forest are named, but their boundaries are not shown.

The map includes two of the Forest lodges, High Lodge and Ranger's Lodge. There were five of these, each associated with one of the five Walks into which the Forest was divided — in the latter part of its existence — to make supervision easier. High Lodge may be medieval in origin, but it is not known when the others were built. Ranger's Lodge is recorded in the 1609 Survey, although known as Batten's Lodge since its occupant at that time was Richard Batten.

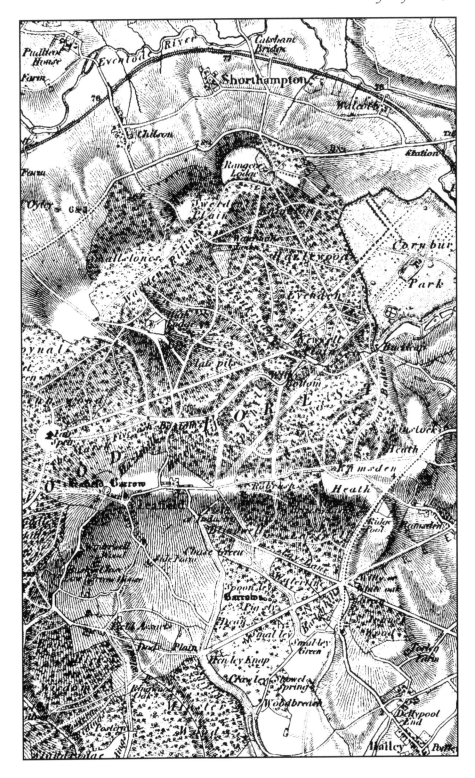

Map 2

The most prominent feature is Lee's Rest Wood (formerly Abbot's Wood) which was the remnant of the woodland of Charlbury and Fawler. It has now almost completely disappeared from the landscape. Dustfield Farm and Harbridge Farm occupy the site of 'the greate common field ... called Dustfield and Abridge' which is also labelled Charlebury Sarte in the 1609 Survey. Presumably the land there also once formed part of Charlbury's 'woodland', although the name Dustfield suggests that it, at least, was a clearing and not densely wooded.

The name Bottom Wood, nearby, is a corruption of Bloxham Wood and this is where the wood belonging to Bloxham manor was situated. It extended through Ash Copse, High Wood and Shire Wood (now Sheer's Copse) and included Kingswood in the northern part of Stonesfield parish.

Holly Grove, below Wilcote, is the Domesday woodland belonging to Wilcote manor, probably unchanged in location and extent since 1086. Topples Wood, north of Wilcote, was not wooded in 1086 but lies over the site of one of Oxfordshire's deserted villages, Tapwell.

In North Leigh Whitehill Wood (near Ashford Bridge) and Sturt Copse, both situated on steep slopes, are the only remnants of the wood measuring $1^1/_2$ leagues by 1 league which was recorded in Domesday Book. It seems very likely that the wood covered the site of the Roman villa there.

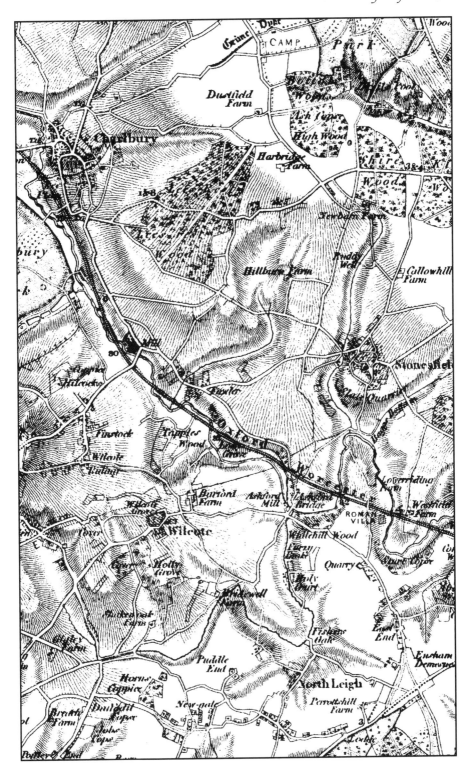

Map 3

The wood shown at the bottom of the map almost certainly formed part of Ducklington's Domesday wood, and it would have been in the Forest immediately before 1219 — but not afterwards, when the river Windrush had been declared a boundary of the Forest. This alteration meant that half of Witney manor (Hailey and Crawley) remained in the Forest, the rest did not.

The common fields of Hailey, which presumably existed in 1086, did not extend north of Higher Farm, Witheridge Cross and Hailey village, and the land to the north of those represents the assarts made in the manor under the influence of its owner, the bishop of Winchester. The woods in the north of Crawley show the typical arrangement of coppices separated by tracks and interspersed with greens. They, and St. John's Wood in Hailey, were not assarted as the bishop kept them as his own Chase (private Forest). This is the reason for the name Chasewood Farm which is now found there.

The adjacent wood is that of Minster Lovell, whose lord was permitted to impark (enclose) it and keep his own deer there in 1442. It too has now been cleared almost completely, as has the wood and heath (Dodd's Plain) to its west and north, which belonged to Asthall.

The hamlet of Field Assarts lies at the boundary between Asthall and Leafield. The land immediately to the north of the hamlet was the site of the woods of Whitele and Purveance, which belonged to Fulbrook before 1307, but when next recorded, in the sixteenth century, the site was occupied by the fields of Purrens, Broad Assarts and Long Assarts, which belonged to Leafield.

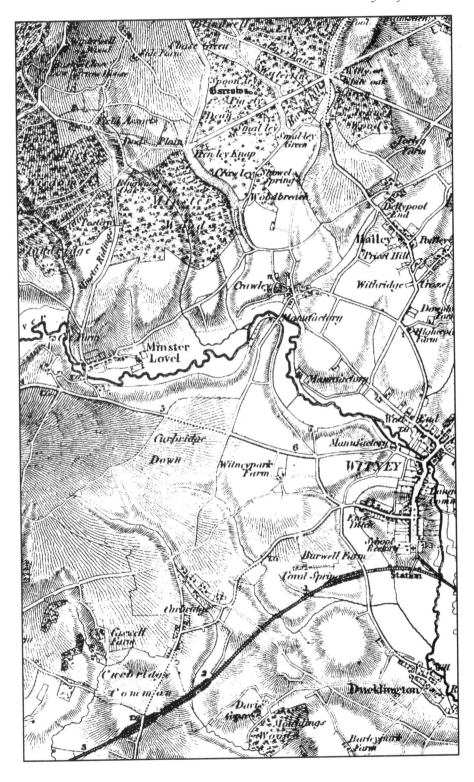

Map 4

Coggs Copse, in the centre of the map, still survives. It was the wood belonging to Cogges manor in 1086, but had a fringe of heath on the southern and western sides, which was later converted to farm land. The blank space above it on the map is Osney Hill, the site of the wood which in 1086 belonged to Kidlington, many miles away to the east.

Woodley Copse and the other grounds surrounding Eynsham Hall, to the right of Coggs Copse, occupy the site of Eynsham's Domesday Wood, which also had a fringe of heath on its eastern and southern sides. The triangle of land named Ensham Demesnes was actually in North Leigh and was part of North Leigh Heath until the Inclosure there in 1759. The heath stretched in a westerly direction to merge with Hailey Common, so that the woods in this area were entirely surrounded by heathland.

The other land in Hailey, shown at the upper left of the map, was probably all assart land. Swanhill Farm is named from the wood of Swaneye, where, it is recorded in the bishop of Winchester's Pipe Rolls, assarts were made between 1249 and 1253.

Tar Wood, at the bottom of the map, was part of the wood belonging to Stanton in 1086, and the rest lay to its right, just below the railway line. The date of its clearance is not known

The woods in this part of the region, belonging to Cogges, Eynsham and Stanton, were sometimes, in the 12th century, treated as a separate Forest called the Forest of Stanton or of Piriho, and the lord of Stanton (Harcourt) manor paid £3 rent for it to the Crown.

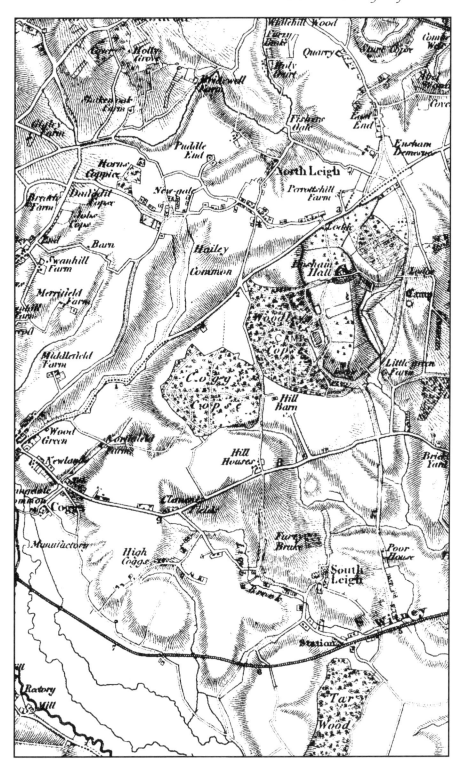

Notes

Introduction

1.   W. G. Hoskins, *The Making of the English Landscape* (1955; Pelican edn, 1970), 44 and 85.
2.   W. G. Hoskins, 'Introduction', in Lionel M. Munby, *The Hertfordshire Landscape* (1977), 23.
3.   Christopher Taylor, *Fields in the English Landscape* (1975),33; H. C. Bowen and P. J. Fowler (eds.), *Early Land Allotment*, BAR 48 (1978), *passim*.
4.   P. H. Sawyer, From *Roman Britain to Norman England* (1978), 132-67.
5.   Oliver Rackham, *Ancient Woodland* (1980), 106.
6.   Rockingham Forest is one example, cited in Malcolm Todd, *The Coritani* (1973), 74.
7.   Oliver Rackham, *Trees and Woodland in the English Landscape* (1976), *passim*; W. J. Ford, 'Some settlement patterns in the region of the Warwickshire Avon', *Mediaeval Settlement, Continuity and Change*, ed. P. H. Sawyer (1976), 274-94.
8.   *The Whichwood Disafforesting Act, 1853;An Act to Amend the Whichwood Disafforesting Act I853, 1856;Declaration of the Boundaries of the Forest and Purlieus as determined by the Commissioners appointed under an Act passed in the 13th year of the reign of Queen Victoria and intituled An Act for Disafforesting the Forest of Whichwood* (Bodleian G.A.Oxon.b 115(1)); Wm.Bryan Wood, Map of the Forest and Purlieus of Whichwood, 1854 (PRO, MR 1682).
9.   The Survey is PRO, LR2/202 fos. 25-49. The background to the Survey is discussed in Phillip A. J. Pettit, *The Royal Forests of Northamptonshire, 1558-1714* (Northamptonshire Record Society, XXIII, 1968), 72-4.
10.   Two versions of the Perambulation exist, one dated 1298 and recorded in the *Eynsham Cartulary*, II, 92-4, and another dated 1300 and reproduced in J. Y. Akerman, 'A view of the ancient limits of the Forest of Wychwood', *Archaeologia*, XXXVII (1857), 435-6. A translation and elucidation of the bounds is given in Beryl Schumer, 'The woodland landscape of the Wychwood region in the centuries before AD 1400' (M. Phil. thesis, University of Leicester, 1980), Appendix I, 158-74.

1. The Wychwood Region

1.   Beryl Schumer, 'The woodland landscape of the Wychwood region in the centuries before AD 1400' (M. Phil. thesis, University of Leicester, 1980), 9-16. Some manors/parishes in the extreme western part of the region had no connection with the woodland and have been omitted from the discussion.
2.   Information used in this section is derived from the Geological Survey of England and Wales, Sheets 218 and 236, Solid with Drift.
3.   A. W. Martin and R. W. Steel (eds.), *The Oxford Region* (1954), 133.

2. Wychwood before 1086

1.   Statements in this chapter for which no reference is given are based on the maps and

record cards of the Sites and Monuments Record at the Centre for Oxfordshire Studies, Oxford Central Library, Oxford.

2.   Don Benson and David Miles, with C. J. Balkwill and N. Clayton, *The Upper Thames Valley, an Archaeological Survey of the River Gravels* (1974), 42-53.

3.   Don Benson, 'Excavations at Ascott-under-Wychwood, Oxfordshire', *Top.* Oxon., XIV (Spring 1969); *Oxoniensia*, XXXII (1967), 72.

4.   Hunphrey Case *et al.,* 'Excavations at City Farm, Hanborough, Oxfordshire', *Oxoniensia* XXIX-XXX (1964-5), 93

5.   J. E. G. Sutton, 'Iron Age hill-forts and some other earthworks in Oxfordshire', *Oxoniensia*, XXXI (1966), 28-42; Nicholas Bayne, 'Excavations at Lyneham Camp, Lyneham, Oxon.', *Oxoniensia*, XXII (1957), 8.

6.   Tim Copeland, 'The North Oxfordshire Grim's Ditch: A Fieldwork Survey', *Oxoniensia,* LIII (1988) 277-292; D.W.Harding,*The Iron Age in Lowland Britain* (1974),74-5.

7.   D. R. Wilson and D. Sherlock, *North Leigh Roman Villa* (D.O.E. Official Handbook, 1980), 7.

8.   Tania M. Dickinson, 'The Anglo-Saxon burial sites of the Upper Thames region and their bearing on the history of Wessex, circa AD 400-700', Bodl. MS D. Phil. C 2124, nos. 144 and 67; *CBA Group 9 Newsletter*, 11 (1981), 138.

9.   Margaret Gelling, *Signposts to the Past* (1978), 126-8. Place-names are included in Map 4 regardless of the date at which they are first recorded, since it is argued later that most, if not all, of them were already in existence in 1086.

10.   *DB Oxfordshire*, 15,3; 28,20, 59,6.

11.   Two *leahs* which do not fit this pattern are Cleveley and Crawley. These discrepancies are so far unexplained.

12.   The name occurs as a boundary point in the charter for Taynton, AD 1059.

3. The Woodland of 1086

1.   *DB Oxfordshire*, 1,5; 1,4; 1,10.

2.   PRO, E36 Bk 75, f.27. The assart was made by John de Langley, the Forester.

3.   Margaret Gelling, *The Early Charters of the Thames Valley* (1979), 132; *Eynsham Cartulary*, II 94; PRO, LR2/202, fos. 34-5;*Rot. Hund.*, II, 867.

4.   PRO, E32/137; LR2/189, f.84.

5.   Wm. Bryan Wood, Map of the Forest and Purlieus of Whichwood, 1854 (PRO, MR 1682); Inclosure Award, Fulbrook, Shipton and Taynton, 1861, PRO MAF 1 338; LR2/202, f.41; Margaret Gelling, 'Pre-Conquest local history: evidence from Anglo-Saxon charters', *Amateur Historian*, I (1952-4), 243-5; *DB Oxfordshire,* 13,1.

6.   H. E. Salter (ed.), *Cartulary of Osney Abbey*, IV (Oxford Historical Society, XCVII, 1934), 136, nos. 97 and 98; PRO, LR2/202, f.29.

7.   Beryl Schumer, 'The woodland landscape of the Wychwood region in the centuries before AD 1400' (M. Phil. thesis, University of Leicester, 1980), Appendix V, 190-1.

8.   *DB Oxfordshire*, 59,21; *Rot. Hund.*, II, 739.

9.   PRO, LR2/189, fos. 78-81.

10.   PRO, E32/137, m.6. John de St Valery's woods then consisted of Westgrove, Losnegrove and East Grove (near Asthall Leigh) and Fastgrove, Small Hok and Farendon. With the exception of Eastgrove, these still belonged to Fulbrook in 1851 (Tithe Award, PRO IR 29 (& 30) /27/62).

11.   PRO C47/11/6 (8); Asthall and Fulbrook were held by the same lord from 1086 until the forfeiture of the Honour of St Valery (to which they then belonged) in 1227.

12.   *DB Oxfordshire* 32,2;*Rot. Hund.*, II, 729, 731,738.

13.   *Rot. Hund.*, II, 729; Schumer, op. cit.,160,170, Appendix IV.

14.   PRO, LR2/202, f.42.

15.   *Cal. Charter Rolls*, VI, p.37. Tithe Award PRO IR 29 (& 30) /27/96.

16.   *DB Oxfordshire*, 28,25; 7,61; 18,2.

17.   PRO, LR2/202 f.34.

18.   Charlbury is not recorded in Domesday Book, being possibly included in the manor of

Banbury. Tithe Award PRO IR 29 (& 30) /27/30; PRO, LR2/202, f.32; E32/137; E32/138.

19.   Charlbury fields were enclosed in 1715, largely in the form of the existing strips which are thus still visible in later maps: VCH Oxfordshire, X (1972), 127; Map of the Charlbury Estates of the Duke of Marlborough, 1761, Bodl. MSC 17: 49(1).

20.   PRO, LR2/202, f.33.

21.   PRO, LR2/202, f.34.

22.   The assarts are recorded in D. Royce (ed.), *Landbuc sive Registrum Monasteriae Beatae Mariae virginis et Sancti Cenhelmi de Winchelcumba* (1892), II, 25-6; *DB Oxfordshire*, 59,14.

23.   PRO, LR2/202, f.33; *Rot. Hund.*, II, 746; BL, Add MS 28024, f.174; PRO, LR2/189, f.68.

24.   *DB Oxfordshire*, 27,4; PRO, LR2/202, f.35, *Eynsham Cartulary*, II, 93.

25.   PRO, LR2/202, f.35; *DB Oxfordshire*, 7,1.

26.   PRO, LR2/202, fos. 36-8; *Osney Cartulary*, ed. Salter, IV, 107, nos. 75-80.

27.   *DB Oxfordshire*,38,1; Bodl.E c 17: 149 (137, 138, 139);*Rot. Hund.*, II, 872.

28.   PRO, LR2/202, fos. 25-9.

29.   *DB Oxfordshire*,3,1.

30.   Patricia Hyde, 'The Winchester manors of Witney and Adderbury, Oxfordshire, in the later Middle Ages', Bodl. MS B.Litt. d 473 (1955), 37.

31.   Beryl Schumer, 'An Elizabethan Survey of North Leigh, Oxfordshire', *Oxoniensia*, XL (1975),22-4.

32.   *Pipe Rolls*, n.s. I, 13, in which North Leigh is Lea Bern'[ardi], from Bernard de St Valery, its lord at that time; PRO, E36, vol.75, f.24 d; *Cal. Patent Rolls*, 1232-1247, 333;*Rot. Hund*, II,868-71.

33.   Schumer, 'Elizabethan Survey',315; 6 acres of assart land in Over Riding is recorded in PRO, SC6 Hen VII 464, a Minister's account for North Leigh.

34.   *DB Oxfordshire*, 29,10; Oxf. Archives, F 17.

35.   This omission may have been due to the fact that this part of the Forest was sometimes treated separately as the Forest of Stanton, or Piriho: *Pipe Rolls*, I, 27; *Pipe Rolls*, V, 25; Pipe Rolls, VI, 47; *Pipe Rolls*, VII, 7.

36.   DB Oxfordshire, 6.6.

37.   *Rot. Hund.*, II,35; V. Wickham Steed, 'Wychwood Forest, its history and management' (typescript, Centre for Oxfordshire Studies, Oxford Central Library), 198.

38.   *VCH Oxfordshire* XII, 128; A sketch version of the map is shown in *Top. Oxon.*, VII (Autumn 1961); *Eynsham Cartulary*, II, 42, no. 609; I, 24-5; E. K. Chambers, *Eynsham under the Monks* (Oxfordshire Record Society, XVIII, 1936), 57.

39.   Field names from the Sites & Monuments Record; H. E. Salter, *Feet of Fines for Oxfordshire*, 1195-1291 (Oxfordshire Record Society, XII, 124, no. 82, and 115, no. 36.

40.   *Cal. Charter Rolls*, I, 1226-1257, p.270.

41.   One hide 'at Hanborough' but belonging to the manor of Stanton was given to Osney Abbey by Adelicia, second wife of Henry I: *Osney Cartulary*, ed. Salter, IV, 107-8, nos. 75, 76, 77, 78, 79.

42.   *DB Oxfordshire*, 7,3;*Rot. Hund.*, II, 855, 856, 872; Tithe Award for South Leigh, PRO IR 29 (& 30) /27/88.

43.   *Rot. Hund*, II, 855.

44.   An account for wastes and assarts in Stanton recurs in the Pipe Rolls between 1185 and II91; *Cal. of Inquisitions*, Henry III, p.111, no. 411.

45.   The same development of the word assart is shown in a Survey of Combe in 1778 (Lincoln College Archives), in which fields known earlier as Old and New Sarte are recorded as Old and New Sate.

46.   *DB Oxfordshire*, 7, 22, 21.

47.   *VCH Oxfordshire* XII, 15; PRO E32/251 m.4d

48.   *Inq. ad Quod Damnum*, part II (PRO Lists & Indexes XXII), 7;*Rot. Hund.*, II,851; PRO LR2/189, f.85.

49.   *Rot. Hund.*, II, 850; *Eynsham Cartulary*, II, 94.

50.   C. J. Bond,'Woodstock Park under the Plantagenet kings: the exploitation and use of wood and timber in a mediaeval deer park', *Arboricultural Journal*, V (1981), 202-3, and James

Bond & Kate Tiller, eds. *Blenheim, landscape for a Palace*, map. p 29.

51. J. Y. Akerman, 'A view of the ancient limits of the Forest of Wychwood', *Archaeologia*, XXXVII (1857), 437; PRO, LR2/202, f.43d.

52. *Pipe Rolls*, XXXIV, 108; n.s. XXX, 20; n.s. X, 225.

53. In some cases it is made clear that acres are to be measured by the Forest perch, or 'by the perch of 20 feet', but in others no such indication is given, and without this it is not possible to know exactly how much land was assarted.

54. J. S. Moore, 'The Domesday teamland, a reconsideration', *Transactions of the Royal Historical Society*, 5th ser., XIV (1964), 109-30.

55. W. D. Campbell, 'The natural history of Wychwood', lecture at Woodstock, 17 October 1981.

56. *Eynsham Cartulary*, I, 25.

57. Thomas Pride, Map of Whichwood Forest, 1787, printed at the end of *Report of the Select Committee on the Woods Forests and Land Revenues of the Crown*, 1848.

58. PRO, LR2/189, f.83; V. Wickham Steed, op. cit., 70.

59. *Journals of the House of Commons*, XLVII 1792), 249.

60. PRO, LR2/202, f.42 ;*Pipe Rolls*, n.s. IV, 245.

61. *Eynsham Cartulary*, II, 95; *DB Oxfordshire*, 28, 25.

62. PRO, LR2/202, f.41, 31.

63. *Eynsham Cartulary*, II, 93 4.

64. PRO, LR2/202, ff. 33d,34; *Eynsham Cartulary*, II, 93.

65. Margaret Gelling, 'English place-names derived from the compound Wicham', *Mediaeval Archeology*, XI (1967),104-5.

4. Settlements and Rights in the Domesday Woodland

1. Frank Emery, *The Oxfordshire Landscape* (1974), 86, plate 7, 102, 143.

2. The best study of these charters is that of Margaret Gelling, in 'English place-names derived from the compound Wicham', *Mediaeval Archeology*, XI (1967), 87-105.

3. *DB Oxfordshire*, 1,5.

4. Map, Inclosure Award for Ramsden township in Shipton-under-Wychwood, Oxf. Archives, bk. 46. A sketch map is given in D. H. Allport, *Ramsden* (1965).

5. The names occur in the Tithe Award for Hailey, PRO IR 29 (& 30)/27/67, and also in early records.

6. Patricia Hyde, 'The Winchester manors of Witney and Adderbury, Oxfordshire, in the later Middle Ages', Bodl. MS B.Litt. d 473 (1955), 294.

7. *Eynsham Cartulary*, I, 139, no . 188.

8. PRO, E32/137.

9. The major Roman sites in the area are shown in Tim Copeland, 'The North Oxfordshire Grim's Ditch', *Oxoniensia* LIII, 1988, 286: A C C Brodribb, A R Hands & D R Walker, *Excavations at Shakenoak V*, pp. 183-5, 205-9. Other information from the Sites and Monuments Record.

10. PRO, LR2/202, f.33. In 1279 (*Rot. Hund.*, II, 709) Fawler consisted of 1 hide 1 virgate held by William le Blund, and 2 fees held by the abbot of Eynsham, of which the Caperun fee had been given to the Abbey in 1213 X 1228 (*Eynsham Cartulary*, I, 410, no. 190) and Danvers fee in 1220 X 1222 (*Eynsham Cartulary*, I, 47, no. 24; 141, no. 192; 143, no. 193; 144, nos. 193a, 194).

11. *DB Oxfordshire*, 3,1.

12. *DB Oxfordshire*, 32,2.

13. T. G. Hassall, review of Emery, The Oxfordshire Landscape, *Oxoniensia*, XL(1975), 333.

14. *DB Oxfordshire*, 56,4; *Rot. Hund.*, II, 734; *Feudal Aids*, IV, 161.

15. Asterleigh is now represented only by Asterleigh Farm. The site of the church and village is recorded in *CBA Group 9 Newsletter*, 10 (1980), pp. 85-6.

16. *Pipe Rolls*, n.s. I, 11. The hamlet was then known as Stantonlega.

17. White Kennett,*Parochial Antiquities* (1695), II, 140;*Rot. Hund.*, II, 855-6.

18. Emery, op. cit.,196;*DB Oxfordshire*, 7,27.

19.   Margaret Gelling, *The Place-names of Oxfordshire*, II (English Place-name Society, XXIV, 1954), 333.

20.   Beryl Schumer, 'The woodland landscape of the Wychwood region in the centuries before AD 1400' (M. Phil. thesis, University of Leicester, 1980), Appendix, V, 188-90.

21.   *Rot. Hund.*, II, 852 (part of Nether Kiddington, including Boriens, is incorrectly described under Combe); ibid., 876, 866, 850; K. J. Allison, M. W. Beresford and J. G. Hurst, *The Deserted Villages of Oxfordshire* (University of Leicester Department of English Local History Occasional Paper 17,1965),32;*CBA Group 9 Newsletter*, 10(1980), 175-7.

22.   *Rot. Hund.*, II, 742, 777; PRO, E32/251.

23.   PRO, LR2/202, f.41. Taynton and Deerhurst had been linked since 1059 when both were given to St Denis, Paris, by Edward the Confessor.;*CBA Group 9 Newsletter*, 10 (1980), 87; V. Wickham Steed, 'Hermitages and Chapels of Wychwood Forest', *Top. Oxon.*, X (Autumn 1963); the hermitage of Lovebury was possibly not on the site of the present Lowbarrow House, but at the near-by Dawn Cottage, which has mediaeval features (personal communication, Mrs. S. F. Sutton).

24.   P. H. Sawyer (ed.), *English Mediaeval Settlement* (1979), 3.

25.   H.A. Evans, *Highways and Byways in Oxford and the Cotswolds* (2nd edn, 1938),377; Alun Howkins, *Whitsun in 19th Century Oxfordshire* (History Workshop Pamphlet no. 8,1973), 15.

26.   PRO, E32/251, E32/137, m. 6d; J. Y. Akerman, 'A view of the ancient limits of the Forest of Wychwood', *Archaeologia*, XXXVII (1857), 437; PRO, C47/11 /8, nos. 22, 27.

27.   *Rot. Hund.*, II, 875, 866, 874.

28.   Ibid., 850.

29.   Vernon J. Watney, *Cornbury and the Forest of Wychwood* (1910), 22. The 'kings' demesne oxen and demesne cows' were allowed in Woodstock Park, and some pigs on payment of pannage, but there seems to have been no general right of common there.

30.   *Journals of the House of Commons* XLVII (1792), 230; Inclosure Award Map of Asthall, 1814, Oxf. Archives, vol. D.

31.   BL. Lansdowne Collection 758, f.16.

32.   Hanborough alone is recorded as raising disputes regarding rights in Eynsham (*Eynsham Cartulary*, II, 104-5); special allotments in lieu of common rights were made for Combe and Stonesfield at the Inclosure of North Leigh, 1759 (Oxf. Archives, F 17); *Rot. Hund.*, II, 850.

33.   *Rot.Hund.*,II,851; G.H.Powell,*Stonesfield* (1975), 15.

34.   Rev. Herbert Barnett, *Glympton, the History of an Oxfordshire Manor* (Oxford Record Society, V, 1923), 23; BL, Add. MS 28024, f.174; *Eynsham Cartulary*, I, 385, no. 564; PRO, E279/161/9.

35.   D. Royce (ed.), *Landbuc sive Registrum Monasteriae ... de Winchelcumba* (1892), II, 209, 205, 206, 207, 208, 210, 170, 211.

36.   PRO, LR2/202, f.34.

37.   Emery, op. cit., 56-7.

38.   *VCH Oxfordshire*, X (1972), 135.

39.   *Eynsham Cartulary*, I, 140, nos. 190, 191; F.N. MacNamara, *Memorials of the Danvers Family* (1895), 58. The Talemasche moiety of the Chevalchesul fee is described both as in Fawler (*Eynsham Cartulary*, I, 144, no. 195) and as in Finstock (*Curia Regis Rolls*, IV, 1205-6, 44); *Rot. Hund.*, II, 709.

40.   PRO, C99/91.

41.   Watney, op. cit., 88.

42.   *Journals of the House of Commons*, XLVII (1792), 230.

43.   PRO, LR2/224, fos. 162-78; LR2/202, f.35.

44.   *VCH Oxfordshire*, X, 141; Elsie Corbett, *A History of Spelsbury* (1931), 79.

45.   Royce (ed.), *op. cit.*, II, 189; Christine Sibbitt, . . . *bells, blankets, baskets and boats* . . . (Oxford City and County Museum Publication no. 1, 1968), 31.

5. Wychwood after 1086

1.   Assarts in Stanton are recorded in 1182 (*Pipe Rolls*, XXXII, 99); in Langley in 1166 (*Pipe Rolls*, XI, 7); in Charlbury probably c.1160 (*Eynsham Cartulary*, I, 54). The other assarts are recorded in *Eynsham Cartulary*, I, 139; *Pipe Rolls*, n.s. I, 13, and *Pipe Rolls*, n.s. X, 226.

2.   *Rot. Hund.*, II,872.

3.   *ibid.*, 868; PRO, E32/137.

4.   Patricia Hyde, 'The Winchester Manors of Witney and Adderbury, Oxfordshire, in the later Middle Ages', Bodl. MS B.Litt. d 473 (1955), 33-4.

5.   *Rot. Hund.*, II, 852; PRO, E36 vol. 75, no. 27; *Rot. Hund.*, II, 872, 967; PRO, C47/11/5 no.4.

6.   PRO, E32/137; *Eynsham Cartulary*, II, 93; *Rot. Hund.*, II, 746; D. Royce (ed.), *Landbuc sive Registrum Monasteriae . . . de Winchelcumba* (1892), II, 25.

7.   PRO, E32/138; LR2/202, f.32; Royce (ed.), *op. cit.*, II, 26 and 206-11; *Cal. Patent Rolls*, 1343-1345, p.379.

8.   'Roots' of wood were sold in Glympton in 1326, implying clearance, not coppicing: Herbert Barnett, *Glympton, the History of an Oxfordshire Manor* (1923), 9.

9.   *VCH Oxfordshire*, IX (1972), 59-60; Shipton was held by Maud, Countess of Clare, by c.1180: A. Clark (ed.), *The English Register of Godstow Nunnery* (Early English Text Society, 1911), 548.

10.   H. M. Colvin, *History of the King's Works* (1963), II, 1009-17.

11.   Brian Paul Hindle, 'The road network of mediaeval England and Wales', *Journal of Historical Geography*, II.3 (1976), 207-21, esp. map, p. 219; William Farrer, *An Outline Itinerary of King Henry the First* (1920), *passim*; PRO, Round Room typescript itinerary of Henry III.

12.   PRO, E32/137, m.5.

13.   Edmund de Wodestoke's assart is recorded in PRO, C47/11/5, and is probably the Old Woodstock Sarte recorded in Wootton in PRO, LR2/202, f.35; the names of Walter of Bladen and John le Turner are found both in the Combe assart (E36 vol. 75 no. 27) and in connection with Woodstock (*Rot. Hund.*, II, 840-1).

14.   *Cal. Close Rolls*, 1227-1231, p.500; Royce (ed.), *op. cit.*, II, 25.

15.   *Eynsham Cartulary*, II, 760, no. 212.

16.   Vernon J. Watney, *Cornbury and the Forest of Wychwood* (1910), 28; references to woodland poducts from Cornbury are found in *Cal. Close Rolls*, Henry III 1231-1234, 75,389; *Cal. Liberate Rolls*, I, 277, 196; II, 42; V, 225. The hurdles were sent to Kenilworth, presumably for use in the siege of Kenilworth Castle.

17.   However, if the Forester exceeded his authority the Forest could be taken from him and returned only on payment of a fine, as happened to Thomas de Langley and John de Langley: *Pipe Rolls*, n.s. IV, 258; *Cal. Close Rolls*, 1307-1313, pp. 384-5.

18.   PRO, E36 vol. 75, f.27; E32/138; *Feudal Aids*, VI (1284-1431), 384.

19.   *Cal. Close Rolls*, 1302-1307, p.323, no. 135.

20.   Josceline Finberg, *The Cotswolds* (1977), 219.

21.   Frank Emery, *The Oxfordshire Landscape* (1974), 87.

22.   E. K. Chambers, *Eynsham under the Monks* (Oxfordshire Record Society, XVIII, 1936), 20.

23.   *DB Oxfordshire*, 6, 6.

24.   *Rot. Hund.*, II, 859-60.

25.   H. C. D. Cooper, 'Eynsham Bounds re-traced', *Top. Oxon.* (Spring 1970).

26.   *Eynsham Cartulary*, I, 134, no.183; 140, nos. 190, 191.

27.   *Pipe Rolls*, n.s. XXIV, 155; n.s. XXX, 20; *Pipe Rolls*, VI, 49; VII, 7; VIII, 67; XI, 11; XII, 204.

28.   Hyde, *op. cit.*,33-4, 87.

29.   *Cal. Charter Rolls*, II, 1257-1300, p.275.

30.   *Cal. Close Rolls*, 1296-1302, p.87; *Cal. Charter Rolls*, VI, p. 37.

31.   *Cal. Patent Rolls*, 1327-1330, p.419.

32.   PRO, E32/137 m.5; *Cal. Inq. Henry III*, 111, no.411.

33.   H. L. Gray, *English Field Systems* (1915, repr. 1959), 84-6 and Appendix III, 510-11.

34.   *Rot. Hund.*, II, 852; PRO, E36 vol. 75, f.27; LR2/202, f.35.

35.   PRO, E32/138; LR2/202, f.32.

36.   *VCH Oxfordshire*, X (1972), 142.

37.   *Rot. Hund*, II, 868-9; Beryl Schumer, 'An Elizabethan survey of North Leigh, Oxfordshire', *Oxoniensia*, XL (1975),314.

38.   PRO, LR2/202, f.25; I. S. Leadam (ed.), *Domesday of Inclosures*, I (1897), 345; Hyde, *op. cit.*, 80; PRO, LR2/202, f.27.

39.   PRO, E32/138; E36 vol. 75, f.27.

40.   *VCH Oxfordshire*, IX, 125.

41.   For example, Trevor Rowley, *The Shropshire Landscape* (The Making of the English Landscape Series, 1972), 97; B. K. Roberts, 'A study of mediaeval colonisation in the Forest of Arden, Warwickshire', *Agricultural History Review*, XVI (1968), 104.

42.   PRO, E32/137.

43.   Six men from North Leigh, two from Ramsden and one from Wilcote held land in the Gatewell Chase assart in Finstock, and men from Ramsden, Finstock, Leafield and Wilcote held land in the assart in the wood of *Lardesleye* in Charlbury manor (PRO, E32/138).

44.   M. M. Postan, *The Mediaeval Economy and Society* (1972, Pelican 1975), 36.

45.   Hyde, *op. cit.*, 246-52.

46.   In Combe, for example, six virgates were each held jointly by two tenants: *Rot. Hund.*, II, 851.

47.   In Taynton, Chadlington, Shipton and Spelsbury the virgate consisted of approximately 40 acres of arable, whereas in North Leigh it was only about 30 acres, and this presumably included the assart land: *VCH Oxfordshire*, II (1907), 192, foot note; PRO, R2/189, f.80; Elsie Corbett, *A History of Spelsbury* (1931), 91; Schumer, *op. cit.*, 312.

48.   *Rot. Hund*, II, 868-70 and 972.

49.   Hyde, *op. cit.*, 285; *Rot. Hund.*, II, 872; PRO, LR2/202, f.35.

50.   The same trend towards small holdings of arable has been found in some other woodland areas; for example, in Arden (J. B. Harley, 'Population trends and agricultural developments from the Warwickshire Hundred Rolls of 1279', *Economic History Review*, 2nd ser. XI, 1958-9, 17), and in Codicote in the Chilterns (David Roden, 'Studies in Chiltern field systems', Ph.D. thesis, University of London, 1965, 159)

51.   *Rot. Hund.*, II, 739.

52.   PRO, E32/137, m.2.

53.   PRO, E32/135; E32/251; E32/137, m.6.

54.   Tenth Report of the Commissioners appointed to Inquire into the State and Condition of the Woods, Forests and Land Revenues of the Crown, *Journals of the House of Commons*, XVII (1792), 250; *Report from the Select Committee on the Woods, Forests and Land Revenues of the Crown* (1848), II, 707-12.

55.   In 1272 the offenders included the abbot of Eynsham and the countess of Gloucester's steward, while the parsons of Kiddington, Eynsham, Charlbury and Great Tew were accused of receiving the venison: PRO, E32/137, m.3.

56.   J. N. Brewer, *The Beauties of Oxfordshire* (1813), 43.

57.   *Cal. of Inquisitions*, IX, 146, no. 139; p.305, no.396.

58.   Hyde, *op. cit.*, 167-80.

59.   *Eynsham Cartulary*, II,29;*VCH Oxfordshire*, X,139,141;PRO, E310/22/210.

60.   Emery, *op. cit.*, 102.

6. The Forest after 1400

1.   PRO LR2/202 ff. 10-11 (p. 33-34).

2.   The annual rent, or *census* of the forest is recorded under the name Cornbury in the Pipe Rolls from 1155 onwards. The name Wychwood first appears there in 1184, but the payment continued to be recorded under Cornbury until *circa* 1470; Charles Johnson and H. A. Cronne, eds., *Regesta Regum Anglo-Normannorum II, 1100-1135*, pp. 43 and 96.

3.   Jennifer Sherwood and Nikolaus Pevsner, *Oxfordshire,* The Buildings of England, pp. 760,

553-4; Vernon J. Watney, *Cornbury and the Forest of Wychwood*, 128.

4.   *VCH Oxfordshire* XII, 433.

5.   The Perambulation is translated and discussed in Beryl Schumer, *The woodland landscape of the Wychwood region in the centuries before AD 1400,* M.Phil. thesis 1980, University of Leicester Appendix I, pp. 158-174; Charles R. Young, *The Royal Forests of Mediaeval England,* 139-147.

6.   Cal. Patent Rolls, 1476-1485, 177.

7.   Edward Marshall, *The Early History of Woodstock Manor and its Environs*, 133; PRO E310/22/120; Watney, *op. cit.* 224.

8.   PRO LR2/189 f.83.

9.   PRO E310/22/120.

10.   An excellent account of this is given in Phillip A J Pettit, *The Royal Forests of Northamptonshire*, Northamptonshire record Society XIII, 50-95. See also *Bernwood, the Life and Afterlife of a Forest*. ed. John Broad & Richard Hoyle, Harris Paper 2, University of Central Lancashire, 1997, p. 56.

11.   *VCH Oxfordshire* XII 434; Sir John Fortescue, Keeper of the Wardrobe and Chancellor to Queen Elizabeth I, was granted Cornbury and the Rangership of Wychwood for life in 1588, and when he died in 1607 the Park and the office passed to his son, Sir Francis Fortescue (Watney, *op. cit.*, 92-3. 97).

12.   BL Add Ms 6027, ff. 49-50, 47.

13.   Marshall, *op. cit.*, 177.

14.   PRO C205 /17 (3); Watney, *op. cit.*, Appendix X.

15.   PRO LR2/189 f. 83; PRO C204/17, transcribed in Watney, *op. cit.,* Appendix VI.

16.   Reports of the Commissioners appointed to Inquire into the State and Condition of the Woods, Forests and Land revenues of the Crown, *Journals of the House of Commons, 1778-1793.* Wychwood is the subject of the 10th Report, *Journals of the House of Commons* 47, 1791-2, 230-264.

17.   Young, A., *A General View of the Agriculture of Oxfordshire,* 1813, 237-8.

18.   *Report of the Select Committee on the Woods, Forests and Land revenues of the Crown,* 1848.

19.   Rayond Grant, *The Royal Forests of England*, 210.

20.   Some of Lord Redesdale's correspondence on the subject is preserved as BL Add Ms 36,649 Vol. XI, pp. 236-240.

21.   For the Disafforesting Acts, see Chapter 1, note 8; The extent of the Forest as stated in the Act was 3742 acres, but other sources quote slightly different figures.

22.   Christine Bloxham, *Portrait of Oxfordshire,* 95-97; Alum Howkins, *Whitsun in 19th century Oxfordshire,* History Workshop Pamphlet No. 8, 1973, 15-18.

23.   Beryl Schumer, *Woodlanders: the village of Leafield, Oxfordshire, and the Pratley family,* University of London thesis for Diploma in the history of the Family, 1991, *passim.*

24.   Oxfordshire Archives Bk 59 (Minster Lovell Allotment, 1861), Bk 31 (Finstock Common Allotment, 1862), Bk 44 (Pudlicote Common Allotment, 1863).

25.   Kate Tiller, "The transformation of Wychwood", *Oxfordshire Local History* Vol. 1 No. 7, 20-22; "The Transformation of Wychwood II" *ibid.* Vol. 1 No. 8, 30-31; Frank Emery, "The transformation of Wychwood: some fresh evidence" *ibid.* Vol. 2, No. 1, 19-22; Beryl Schumer, "More on the origin of Fordwells" *ibid.* Vol. 2 No. 2, 56-59.

26.   Frank Emery, *The Oxfordshire Landscape*, 160.

27.   The experiences of a man who took up one of the new farms (although not immediately after its creation) are described in *Rain and Ruin, the Diary of an Oxfordshire Farmer John Simpson Calvertt 1875-1900*, ed. Celia Miller.

28.   C. Belcher, "On reclaiming the Waste lands as instanced in Wichwood Forest", *Journal of the Royal Agricultural Society of England* 24 (1863), 281

7. Re-writing the History

1.   W.G. Hoskins and L. Dudley Stamp, *The Common Lands of England and Wales* (1963), 9.

2.   Margaret Wilson, 'The Warwickshire Avon', *English Mediaeval Settlement*, ed. P. H. Sawyer (1979), 150- 1.

4.   Hooke, *op. cit.*, 56.

5.   The mosaics of the villas at North Leigh and Stonesfield are ascribed to the school of Corinium (Cirencester).

6.   Shimon Applebaum, 'The agriculture of Shakenoak Villa', in A. C. C. Brodribb, A. R. Hands and D. R. Walker, *Excavations at Shakenoak* V (1978), 196; C. L. Cram, 'Animal bones', *ibid.*, 117-60.

7.   It is perhaps of interest that the field which contains the site of the Ditchley villa was described as 'land', not 'wood', in 1300, and that the site of Callow Hill villa was 'Bentleye', implying a clearing, in contrast to the adjacent woods. This suggests that some at least of the villa sites may have been kept open, presumably by grazing.

8.   A map of the Oxford region in Roman times appears as fig. 27 in A. F. Martin and R. W. Steel (eds.), *The Oxford Region* (1954), and the distribution of sites shown there has not been significantly changed by more recent discoveries. Both that map and map 13 show a similar curious gap between the Swalcliffe-Bloxham area and Wychwood, as if that area was cleared and settled, but of no great importance.

9.   Bloxham was the head of a Hundred, held prior to 1066 by the earl of Mercia, and after that date by the king: *VCH Oxfordshire*, IX (1972), 58-9. Swalcliffe was a large parish containing several small separate settlements, most of which belonged to the bishop of Lincoln's Banbury estate, and were presumably an early royal gift to the bishopric (originally of Dorchester): *VCH Oxfordshire*, X (1972), 229.

10.   A small Roman site has been found in Shipton but nothing to suggest that it was a major settlement: Frank and Margaret Ware, 'Practical Fieldwalking in the Evenlode Valley', *Wychwoods History* No. 4, 1988, pp. 42-44. The Roman settlement near Chipping Norton is shown in Kirsty Rodwell (ed.), *Historic Towns in Oxfordshire, A Survey of the New County* (1975), 89.

11.   Rhona M. Huggins, 'The significance of the place-name *Wealdham*', *Mediaeval Archeology*, XIX (1075), 198-201. Waltham occurs as a place-name in Kent, Sussex, Hampshire, Berkshire, Essex, Leicestershire and Lincolnshire.

12.   Alan Everitt, 'River and Wold', *Journal of Historical Geography*, III.1 (1977), 1-19; Della Hooke, 'Early Cotswold woodland', *Journal of Historical Geography, IV.4 (1978)* 333-41; T. R. Slater, 'More on the Wolds', *Journal of Historical Geography*, V.2 (1979), 218. The development of the wolds from the *wald* of the early Saxon period raises the problem of why Wychwood, and Rockingham Forest in Northamptonshire, remained as woodland while the nearby Cotswolds, and Bromswold, were cleared.

13.   E. P. Witney, *The Jutish Forest, A Study of the Weald of Kent from 450-1380 AD* (1976), *passim*, but especially pp. 96 and 69; Peter Brandon, *The Sussex Landscape*, (1974), 72-3

14.   David Roden, 'Studies in Chiltern field systems' (Ph. D. thesis, University of London, 1965), 61,63,90.

15.   The coppices were enclosed for the first seven years after cutting 'for the salvation of the spring', but were then thrown open for grazing.

16.   Chandos Sydney Cedric Brudenell Bruce, 7th marquess of Ailesbury, *The History of Savernake Forest* (1962), 3; Phillip A.J. Pettit, *The Royal Forests of Northamptonshire, 1559-1714* (Northamptonshire Record Society, XXIII,1968) 7 and map I

17.   Charles R. Young, *The Royal Forests of Mediaeval England* (1979), 15; F. H. M. Parker, 'Inglewood Forest', *Transactions of the Cumberland & Westmorland Antiquaries and Archaeological Society*, n.s. X (1910), 7.

18.   D. V. Fowkes, 'The breck system of Sherwood Forest', *Transactions of the Thoroton Society*, LXXXI (1977), 55-6.

19.   Alan Everitt, 'The Wolds once more', *Journal of Historical Geography*, V.1 (1979), 71

Index

(The maps and tables have not been indexed)

About the Wychwood Press

The Wychwood Press publishes books of local interest, particularly (though not exclusively) of relevance to the area of the Oxfordshire Cotswolds within the medieval royal forest of Wychwood. This is an area loosely bounded by the towns of Witney, Woodstock, Chipping Norton and Burford, and includes the valleys of the Evenlode and Windrush.

Our first books are the present volume, together with a new edition of John Kibble's *Wychwood Forest and its Border Places*.

Forthcoming titles will include, we hope, re-issues of John Kibble's other works, including *Charlbury and its Nine Hamlets: Chadlington, Chilson, Coate, Fawler, Finstock, Pudlicote, Shorthampton, Tappewell, and Walcot, with Spelsbury* (to include Jesse Clifford's *My Reminiscences of Charlbury*, written in 1891-1892: Clifford was headmaster of the British School in Charlbury from 1842 to 1884); *The History of Charlbury* by Lois Hey; and an updated and abridged edition of Vernon Watney's rare work, *Cornbury and the Forest of Wychwood*, presently being undertaken by Charles Tyzack. We also plan a book of art and craft as practised in the area today.

We welcome ideas for further titles, and will be glad to hear your suggestions. Please write to Jon Carpenter at The Wychwood Press, 2 The Spendlove Centre, Charlbury OX7 3PQ, or phone or fax 01608 811969. We will be happy to add you to our mailing list for advance information about new titles as they are published.